To mom

Xmas '76

Gladys & Alice

A Welsh Country Parson

By the same author

Welsh Country Upbringing
Welsh Country Characters

D. PARRY - JONES

A Welsh Country Parson

B. T. Batsford Ltd
London and Sydney

Dedicated
to the memory of my wife
who was with me
for fifty of the sixty years
covered in this book

© D. Parry-Jones 1975
First published 1975

ISBN 0 7134 2916 X

Computer typeset by Amigo Graphics Centre Ltd
21 Mt Ephraim Road, Tunbridge Wells, Kent
Printed in Great Britain by
Tinling (1973) Limited, Prescot, Lancs
for the Publishers B T Batsford Limited
4 Fitzhardinge Street London W1H OAH
and 23 Cross Street, Brookvale, NSW 2100, Australia

Contents

ONE

Ordination

———————◦———————

IN THE FIRST VOLUME, *Welsh Country Upbringing,* I traced
briefly my life up to the day I left college. In that volume,
too, I referred to the barren periods in my life: such a period I
was to experience between leaving college and my ordination.
Had I been properly advised, had there existed a body that
took an interest in ordinands, I should have been directed to
a theological college, but in default of such interest, and such
a body, I whiled away my time at home. It is true that I was
for ever reading and widening my mental horizon, but much
of it was unguided reading, apart from the books set for the
Deacon's examination. I took Sunday duties in my native
parish and worked like an unpaid Lay Reader. Doubtless, it
was a splendid experience, in that, amongst other things, it
accustomed me to facing a congregation, and getting me well
over my stage-fright. In time there came the question of a
curacy, for it may not be known amongst lay people that no
bishop will ordain a young man unless he can find a 'title', i.e,
a parish priest willing to take him. It was over this that I first
disagreed with my parents, and made a stand for an idea that
I had formed myself. It seems that a kindly neighbour had a
friend, or a relative, a Vicar in North Wales, who very much
needed a curate, but in those days North Wales produced in
my mind nothing but visions of mountains, mists, lonely
churches and a scattered population, so I refused to entertain
the idea for one moment, and gave my reason. It had been
borne in on me by that time that my experience of life was
very limited: home, school and college, all in rural settings. I
knew that beyond my small circle there was a huge,

pulsating, moving world, and into this world I was determined to plunge. I was young, healthy and strong, and indeed
was anxious for work and adventure. I believed, as every
young man should at the commencement of his career, that I
could do big things, and to do big things one had to get a big
stage, and though the big things have not been accomplished,
I am sure that those who have known me will not deny that I
tried, and that I worked hard. I knew no other way of
working — I had seen no other way. My parents belonged to
the farming community who worked all the hours of daylight
and at the anxious times of haymaking and the corn harvest
often put in very strenuous labour, for in that way only, in
unsettled weather, could they save their crops. I remember
one of my early Vicars excusing himself to a parishioner for
some omission or other by putting it down to 'pressure of
hard work'. I was shocked, for work to me was work as my
father worked and as the community in which I had been
brought up worked.

I should have stated, in view of the interval that lay ahead
of me that I tried to get a post as a teacher, and registered
myself with a firm of London agents who specialised in
finding posts for such as myself. I believe that their payment
was a certain percentage of the first year's salary. I explained
to them my capabilites and outlined my requirements. They
sent me many batches of advertisements, practically all from
private schools in this country and in Ireland. Some were run
under the auspices of The Church of England, one, I
remember, under that of the Quakers. They were mostly
small schools, of course, but one thing characterised them all:
the paucity of the pay they offered. It is true they all offered
board and residence, but anxious as I was to fill up the
interval and do something, I had to turn them all down for
the wages offered would hardly pay my train fare. This must
have been a dreadful field of cheap and sweated labour.
Allied to no organisation or union, the lot of the young men
who filled these obscure and junior posts in these private
schools must have been a deplorable one. I wonder if it is so
today, and if so, how long they are to remain outside
government inspection and legislation. It was better to
remain at home on the farm and regard it all as a very long

vacation. Indeed it was very pleasurably spent, and I think, too, very profitably spent. There were long holidays to many relatives, there were the seasonal activities in the fields at which I assisted, there were the horses, and above all there was the abundant leisure for my studies which were my first love.

One day I met an old college friend, who, having been ploughed in his final examination, was recuperating in the Rhondda, and taking, meanwhile, a course of Lay-reading as a remedial aid, in the parish of Pontypridd. It seems the new Vicar there required a Welsh-speaking curate. After some correspondence I had an interview and was accepted. This brought great excitement to my bosom. I was to start my life's work; my first sphere was already marked out for me. I was about to plunge forth into the big, throbbing world that I knew existed, and the Rhondda to me then was certainly big and certainly throbbing. The salary was to be £130 per annum, a sum that was considered to be very satisfactory indeed. Some were offering as low as £120. Then the Bishop of Llandaff in whose Diocese I had been given the title wished to know before he accepted me what sort of character I bore, and what sort of qualifications I had. As to the former I had my own parish priest and two other priests to testify to my blameless life. As to the latter question I could only refer him to my college Principal. In both these matters there was nothing to explain, and I had no anxiety on that score. Then finally there came the '*Si Quis*' − from the opening Latin phrase ('if anyone'). This was a document to be read in the parish church at the time of Divine Service, inviting anybody in the congregation to declare whether they knew of any thing in my life that rendered me unfit for Orders in the church, as I had sought admission to the same. This is a very old practice and can very well be as old as trial by jury. For it was a trial − a trial by my own peers, the men and women who knew me and my parents. Those who had played with me, and those with whom I had worked in the harvest fields − the verdict remained entirely in their hands. Would they acquit me and show their approval of me by remaining seated and silent? It reminds me in some respects of the calling of banns before marriage, in which the parishioners are invited to declare whether they know of any just cause or impediment why the two persons should not be joined together in Holy Matrimony. And I was about to be wedded to the church 'Until death do us part', for once a priest always a priest. I like the old-world atmosphere that surrounds many of the acts of the church. It is certainly democratic and that without knowing it, for though ordination is from above, through the bishops, final acceptance is in the hands of the people.

It is remarkable how very much more interest was taken in the young man who was preparing himself for the ministry than in anyone entering any other profession, say the medical, the legal or the teaching profession. Many of my neighbours, even though they were not church people, came to hear me preach when it was learnt that I had started. They judged kindly I know, but shrewdly too. Their verdict was not based so much on actual show as upon promises and possibilities, i.e, what gifts of delivery, voice, etc. I had.

As part of my preparation, I had to go and see the family tailor, who on the strength of his London experience in his early days, advertised himself, amongst other things, as a clerical and military tailor. He certainly rigged me out in all that I required. One of the requirements was a frock-coat suit, the clergy having ceased to wear the cassock as the outdoor habit; it included a vest waistcoat buttoning up the side. In addition there was the soft, 'pancake' or 'Jim Crow' hat, and the round collar. With the rest of my brethren I have long discarded all but the clerical collar and I shall not be sorry when that goes too. I have often felt I should like to adopt the neck-wear prevalent in the eighteenth and early part of the nineteenth century in which the old clergy looked so distinctive and dressy, i.e, clerically so. However, there is a lot to be said for the pancake hat and the round collar, for they do mark one out as belonging distinctly to a separate order, and I remember well the awed feeling that came over me when I first beheld myself in the mirror thus habited. It does help one to realise that he no longer quite belongs to himself, but must now tread warily, as so many eyes are upon him, and be prepared willingly to offer help and immediate involvement in the troubles of anyone who approaches him, utterly disregarding his own personal convenience. There is a tendency amongst high-church clergy to go back to the cassock, but it has obvious drawbacks: it soon becomes very dusty and dirty and puts a restriction upon free, vigorous movement. A distinctive badge would serve best of all.

From the moment I had a request from the Bishop of Llandaff for three references as to my character, official cognisance had been taken of me, and I 'officially' existed as a member of the church, and indeed as one who might be of use to the church, provided I passed my Deacon's examination, which I fortunately did. If I had failed, I should probably have had recognition withdrawn, to go back once more to obscurity and oblivion. However, since I did pass, it became my lot to meet the church officially. I went into retreat for the ordination, met the examiners and had an interview with the bishop. And I must say that I found the church 'officially' very nice and very concerned. Indeed I was almost made to feel that I and my career had been its profoundest concern all along. The Ordination took place at St Mary's Church, Abergavenny, as the Bishop's Palace, including the chapel, had been burnt down. Here I saw first Dr Barnes, one of the examiners, later bishop of Birmingham, and was very much impressed by his tall, studious, ascetic appearance, and by all that he told us. After 60 years, much of the scene is blurred and many of the impressions faded, and whether the bishop (Bishop Hughes of Llandaff) pressed his hands hard upon my head, I don't know, but I can still recall what I imagine to be that pressure to this day – hands with the past heavy on them, hands that reached back to St David and St Peter, and I was made a deacon. One thing I should have liked, and that was to have my parents with me to witness my Ordination. Their cup would have been full. But as it came at a busy time and took place at a considerable distance, that joy was denied them, and denied me, too. Our Ordination morning was the first time for us to put on the full clerical attire and walk out in it, and I well remember the mild shock I had when I saw for the first time my college friends dressed up as priests. We were all somewhat self-conscious and awkward, and imagined that everybody was looking at us, as at some strange phenomenon, but once we found ourselves in our parishes and amongst strangers, this soon wore off, and in a very short time we felt as if we had been priests for years. I suppose something of the same self-conscious feeling is experienced by a policeman the first time he walks down the street in his uniform.

TWO

First Appointment: The Rhondda

THE ORDINATION OVER, I made for my new parish — St Catherine's, Pontypridd. Lodgings had been found for me, inspected by me, and certain luggage had been sent on. Lodgings were a new experience to me; what in my inspection I looked for I don't know, apart from looking to see if there was a fireplace there, a table, a chair and a bookcase. As this minimum. had proved ample for me for three years in my college rooms, I was satisfied. It seemed all right, but it wasn't all right, as I soon began to discover. Good lodgings demand more than just ample furniture. The two sisters who owned the house were diminutive creatures, made up mostly, it would seem, of material that periodically exploded into violent shouting and quarrelling. For the first month or so they managed to keep it suppressed and under control, but strange sounds began to invade my room, made up at first of hisses which gradually assumed a human quality, coming evidently through compressed lips. Soon the mounting hatred and anger could not be contained within compressed lips, but exploded into words — and violent words at that! Consideration for the peace of the lodger could no longer be allowed to interfere with a family quarrel, much less put an end to it — to blazes with him, hisses and suppressed words had to be released or else something within would burst. The eldest sister did apologise to me one day for these outbursts, but what I said in return I have clean forgotten. Occasionally a retired nonconformist minister came in, undoubtedly in the endeavour to bring peace, but it invariably ended in a fiercer altercation than before. I lived on there, however, for the best part of a twelvemonth, then moved to another lodgings, found for me by the good mothers of the church, where I discovered what good lodgings, with peace, cleanliness and kindness meant. One of the first impressions I had in my new life and work was how kind and friendly the average church family was. There were certain homes which the junior clergy visited frequently and regularly and where they were cordially and sincerely welcomed. Often they were families who had a son or a close relative in the ministry, but there were many others, who could claim no personal relationship with the ministry, who welcomed the young clergy equally sincerely, and showed a genuine interest in their welfare and happiness, often enquiring about their lodgings, the cooking, and so forth. It was through the active concern of such mothers that I found my new lodgings. On the whole, young clergy in the church of England do not lack good friends willing and anxious to help them and that out of genuine regard for their comfort and out of respect for them as ministers of the church. It is often said that young clergy are the easy and ready prey of match-making mothers. Conceited young men may think that is the case, but I fancy that the reverse is the truth, and that when a mother discovers the first signs of infatuation — generally shown in the weakening, or breakdown, of the resistance to having to go to church twice on Sunday, in addition to going to Sunday School in the afternoon, it could even be accompanied by an offer to take a Sunday school class — when she sees this, she calls her daughter aside and tells her the stark, naked facts of life, that is, facts as they affect a clergyman's wife. She will be told that she will have to live on very little money, that she will have to put up with a lot of very awkward people, that her home will not be ever entirely her own, but that other people will claim the right to call there at any time of the day and bring their problems with them. If she still persists, she will be warned that of course she is making her own bed — largely made up of these and other prickly facts of life — and she must lie on it. I don't think my wife had any surprises when she married a clergyman.

One thing my wife was determined not to be was the *typical* parson's wife. Very few parishes today have any idea what sort of person the *typical* parson's wife was, for the type was on the way out when we got married. By *typical,* I think the majority meant the *bossy* type, the wife who bossed her husband and bossed the parish and everybody in it — a Mrs Proudie, of Barchester Towers' fame. Trollope, in his portraiture of Mrs Proudie, must have done much to kill the type. As far as my knowledge of parsons' wives goes, the typical is the one who remains in the background, quietly and courageously running a big house on small money, watching carefully the health of her husband so that he can keep going and do his work, for if he breaks down, they are in dire trouble, for there are not many sources where they can look for help, and the help that is offered is only on a very limited scale. But if this does not happen, she continues to play her part in the life of the parish, doing good often by stealth.

Today there is emerging a very different type of parson's wife, a person not often seen by the parishioners, for she is out at work all day, and the parish has to do most of the things which at one time were quietly and unobtrusively done by the Vicar's wife. It is possibly a very good thing for the parish.

Before we were led astray to talk about parsons' wives, I was talking about the kindness young clergy invariably receive from church families, but I must now return to my new parish. After my Ordination I went straight there, arriving a few days before Christmas, but I was not asked to do much that day apart from reading the epistle and helping at the distribution at the Communion Service. I paid, I know, a visit to the Sunday school. Besides me, the parish boasted a staff of Vicar, two other curates, a Church Army sister and two Lay Readers. No parish in Wales, or England either, will ever be manned on this scale again. I immediately began to cultivate the friendship of my two colleagues, for there was much I wanted to know, and I preferred to show my ignorance to them rather than to my Vicar. They willingly answered all my questions and put me right on many things. I owed much to them for one never saw the Vicar except at our meetings on Monday mornings. These two curates were in charge of districts of their own, each with its own mission church. I, on the other hand, did the visiting in the older and narrower streets of the town which belonged to the area of the parish church. The Vicar very nicely and kindly one day told me, as he swept his hand over the residential area where the prosperous and the wealthier families of the town lived, that he would hold himself responsible for that part, but he would be surprised if he knew how often I visited those homes, invariably at the invitation of the families.

I at once came face to face with a problem unique to the Welsh church: that of bilingual services. On my first Sunday in the parish, I had to take a Welsh service. We had our morning service in the parish church at 10.00 am so as to be out in time for the normal English mattins to be held at eleven. It was not a satisfactory arrangement. In the evening we met in the church room. The parish had a Welsh congregation, but not a Welsh church. The congregation was made up almost entirely of aged and middle-aged people whose homes were scattered over a wide area of the town. They were folks of dual loyalty: very loyal to their church and very loyal to their language, but they laboured under the conviction that, having no church of their own, they were regarded as second-class members and were accounted of very little importance; indeed, were regarded as a source of nuisance to those who ran the parish, and that it could be run very much more smoothly and economically if they did not exist.

It was an awkward and delicate situation: and things were not improved when it was discovered that the new vicar was a monoglot Englishman. The senior curate, Mr Gabriel, had enough Welsh to take the services, but not to preach. The existence of two languages, spoken side by side, inevitably brings problems, especially so when the weaker, the scorned, is the ancient, native tongue of the country, but swamped by the sudden and heavy inrush of English immigrants. English people might perhaps understand better the soreness felt by Welsh people if we ask them to imagine what their reaction would be, for example, in Gloucestershire, if they found their homeland overrun by a horde of monoglot Welsh immigrants from Monmouthshire when it was Welsh-speaking, and who, as their number and power increased, appropriated to themselves all the parish churches and their endowments, leaving the few pockets of loyalists to build once again churches for themselves and secure maintenance for their own ministry — a minority, and second-class citizens in their own country.

The Vicar — The Rev. Watkins Edwards — was a friendly person and well-disposed towards the Welsh congregation. He did his best to maintain the Welsh services; he certainly did as much for them as did his Welsh-speaking predecessor. The Welsh congregation had no grievance against him at all, but, I suppose, like most English people, he could not understand why, in view of the fact that they could understand English, they did not join the English congregation and so solve one of the greatest problems of the parish.

The English church and the English government were let off very lightly in the case of their nationals who came in such large numbers to Wales, in that they had not to provide one penny in building places of worship, in providing religious services or educational facilities for them, nor indeed to feel any anxiety for their moral welfare. But in the case of those who emigrated to North America, Australia and New Zealand, they had to build churches and schools for them, and supply ministers and teachers at very considerable expense. Similarly, in the case of those who found themselves on the continent, in the pursuit of trade, or filling government posts, churches had to be built for them too, and chaplains provided. Wales provided everything free of charge. We could have refused to do it as our Christian forbears refused to help in the evangelisation of the Saxons at the invitation of St Augustine. To our credit this time we did not refuse, but it cost us much and it left us with many problems.

We, on the other hand, when our people settle in their thousands, as they have done, in Liverpool, Manchester, Bristol and London, have to see that churches and chapels are built for them and that an adequate ministry is provided for them. They could perish for all that any parish priest in any of these large towns, as far as I ever heard, cared for them. We are not grumbling about this. I never met any Welshman who ever expected anything else. I am merely noting the difference.

Fortunately most of the immigrants were members of the Church of England and were readily absorbed. Had it been otherwise, they would not have found Welsh Nonconformity so accommodating — until they saw the inevitability of the *Inglis côs* (English cause). They slowed down very considerably the advance of anglicisation in South Wales, but in doing so had to pay a heavy price — the inevitable price of holding on to a language and its dependent culture when they were being gradually but surely undermined. But it is a gallant chapter in their history, and they deserve a warmhearted tribute for their loyalty. Even to this day their Welsh chapels in the valleys and towns of South Wales are a line of bastions and bulwarks defending the frontiers of the language.

The Welsh church at this time was much more accommodating, but we must remember that it was the time of the alien bishops (*Esgyb Eingl*) and when we began in the latter part of the century to get Welsh bishops, they were, apart from Bishop Hughes of St Asaph, sons of the smaller gentry who, by upbringing, education and association, were far more English than Welsh — English in culture and leanings with a poor command of the language, and not much love for it. English clergy without knowledge of the vernacular, or with very superficial knowledge if it were appointed to parishes where the services were in Welsh. During this period many Welsh services were discontinued far too soon and without sufficient reason. In the present climate of thinking, and in the awakened awareness that so much of our cultural heritage has come down to us through the vernacular, few, if any, priests would be prepared today to 'drop' their Welsh services. This appears to be a post-glacial period as far as the Anglican church is concerned and in the present pervasive warmth, many of our young clergy are making efforts to master the language, realising that we all are members of a bilingual church.

I was led to this digression as I wanted to describe what happened in the parishes when, in its later stages, the volume of immigration proved more than the native community could absorb, as it had been able to up till then. Some of our most loyal Welsh families in South Wales bear such names as

Smith, Mainwaring, Heycock; indeed the whole gamut of English surnames may be found in South Wales, many of them amongst the diaconate of the Welsh chapels. But to return to my Vicar, he must have wondered why my congregation, as they were all conversant with English and well able to join in an English service, did not do so, and save so much duplication. It is a big question, and to answer it adequately would require a whole chapter, nevertheless within the compass of two or three paragraphs the attempt has to be made.

It is not sheer cussedness or contrariness that influences a Welshman in asking for Welsh services or in endeavouring to provide Welsh services for himself and his family, and it is certainly not due to any pleasure that he gets, or is supposed to get, in boycotting an English service just because it is in English. He loves his language and he loves his country; when he emigrates he cannot take his country with him, but he can take his language, and outside Wales it is the only bit of the homeland left to him, and he treasures it all the more. In the use of the Welsh language in a Welsh service, a thousand memories, with their associated emotions, return to him from early years. A Welsh hymn to him is not merely a hymn, it brings with it the whole congregation of that little Bethel where he used to sing it. So much of the rural life of Wales centred round the places of worship and their week-day activities, that the first thing a Welshman does when he finds himself away from home, is to organise his friends and acquaintances into a congregation and build a chapel. So there comes to life once more a little bit of the Wales that he knew, and he is happy again.

Language is much more than an instrument or tool devised for a certain purpose. For example, when one wants to hit a nail in, one uses a hammer, or when one wants to cut down a tree one uses an axe, so when one wants to convey orders, information or testimony one uses words; but language is very much more than a sequence of words as they come off the tongue or the typewriter. As spoken by another human being they carry emphasis here and there, and as the occasion demands can come charged with emotion, sympathy, sorrow or joy. I defy any Welsh bard to weave *galar* or a word of similar sounds into a gay, happy, lively verse, and similarly any English poet to do the same with *woe*. So much of the pain and the suffering endured, and so much of the joy and pleasure experienced, by our early ancestors have gone to the making of our language. 'Its rhythms have been made to sing, weep, soothe, mock, storm, flatter, exhort or reason for maybe a thousand years'.[1]

'Old languages with fine literary traditions, rich in emotion and thought — their every word possessing a long life-history, pregnant with deep and varied associations — are obviously more powerful than new languages' and, of course, than newly acquired languages.[2]

Welsh-speaking people could not explain their feeling and preference in this way, and in these terms, but it is something like this that is behind their stand.

Had the immigration of the nineteenth century gone in reverse, that is, had surged over the border into Gloucestershire and made dominant this alien tongue and culture, there would have been found, I am sure, pockets of resistance amongst the English people who would have made a similar stand, not out of blind stubbornness, but for reasons identical with those I have described above.

It was a new experience for a young man, and one that gave considerable pleasure, whose life so far had been that of a student, much under the guidance and direction of others, to find himself on Ordination being looked up to and in a small way consulted, if only by small people and over small matters, but still consulted. He was the recipient of a few confidences from his Vicar, revealing the seamy side of some folks, outwardly quite respectable, and he began to marvel at the profound knowledge a parish priest has of his people, and the many secrets he carries in his head. Now and again I was commissioned to carry out a few delicate and important missions. I realised that my office and profession gave me considerable importance as an individual. I counted at last, if only in a small area of an industrial valley; it might be nothing to brag about, but it did not come about unnoticed

1. *Language in History* by Harold Goad (Pelican Books)
2. Ibid, p.19

by one who up to that time had not counted for much anywhere, or so it seemed. I was no longer a student whose life and activity in the main consisted of attending lectures, taking down notes, putting in a minimum of four *chapels* a week and sitting my examinations. A full church listened attentively to what I said from the pulpit. Truly Ordination had wrought a great and sudden change in my status. Questions of doctrine and church policy were broached in order to have my opinion.

When I travelled by train and found myself in a compartment of working men, invariably one of them would, with an outward show of diffidence and with deep respect, ask me to enlighten him on a matter — a Biblical matter — that had puzzled him all his life, and apparently had shattered, or nearly shattered a promising Christian life: 'Where did Cain get his wife from?' He had, he said, read that story many a time, and he explained to me that the Bible clearly declares that Adam and his family were the first and only people on the face of the earth. I could only explain it on the hypothesis that there were other people than the Adam family in existence at the time, and yet what right had I to assume that this was so when the Bible gives us no warrant to believe any such thing. My only justification for the theory, or assumption, was that it was the only way in which it could be explained.

In another compartment at another time I would be asked to explain how the blowing of trumpets could bring down the walls of Jericho. Others were worried, or so they appeared to me, over their inability to reconcile the biblical story of creation with the now universally accepted theory of Charles Darwin, worked out in his *Origin of Species*. I knew very little about evolution in those days and had never read the *Origin of Species*, and so, for safety's sake, kept to Genesis. I knew that theory. Considerable help had been given to us in College, in our study of the Old Testament, on this matter, and I proceeded to explain to him that 'days' could stand for quite considerable periods of time. I did my best to close the gap between Darwin and Genesis. But as it turned out that in all such compartments and amongst all such men, the same questions were always fired at me, I discovered that they were the stock questions of a certain type of person — one who had been brought up in Sunday School and who had dabbled much in religion — and fired at young clerics merely to embarrass and entangle them.

I learnt early the value of visiting, and was given a district to cover and bring a report in the following Monday morning when the whole staff met at the Vicarage. I kept a book in which I recorded all my visits, with details of the number of communicants in the families, the number in Sunday School, and so on, everything that I thought it would be useful to have a record of, including, in the case of those who had lapsed, their explanations of how it came about. Sometimes it was blamed on the church itself, or on the clergy — poor grandmother had been dead and buried a month before the Vicar got to know about it. In time my way of dealing with such cases was to assume that she died without the help or knowledge of the doctor either. 'Oh, no, the doctor attended her most assiduously'. One's next question was: 'How did he find out?' People are most unreasonable. In all my parishes, I worked with clergy who believed in visiting.

During one of my early months, visiting an elderly man, I was asked to make a will. I knew nothing about wills, but the request was made to me as if I did know all about them, and I had naturally to pretend that I did. I heartily wished that some elementary information about the making of wills had been given us, say in our last year in college, if only the warning that wills be better left alone. Fortunately for me, I was not asked to make it there and then, but the following week. The first thing I did was to seek out the senior curate, not willing to show my ignorance in the matter to my Vicar. He very kindly showed me the important points to watch, and recommended the buying of a printed form where much of the formal matter was already supplied. The day arrived and the Will was drawn up with the help of the printed form. I have used 'fortunate' with regard to this will before, and I will use it again for I was fortunate in that it was a simple will, mostly sharing out amongst the children the furniture of the home; had there been an article like escritoire, I am sure I should have been floored. Neighbours were brought in to sign it, and I felt, indeed was made to feel, that I was an

important person. For this service, I was given my first gift —
a dozen eggs. Realising that I had to be a bit of a lawyer as
well as a priest, I bought a most useful book called 'Law for
the Millions', and never had much difficulty after that in
making wills. But in time I began to refuse to make wills if I
thought the family could afford to pay the solicitor his very
moderate charge for doing it. I was early given the advice,
which I strictly acted upon and which I passed on to others,
never to make a will where property, however small, is
concerned. It is a lawyer's job and it is best for the clergy to
keep to their own work. I have known cases where clergy
have become very unpopular with church families for no
other reason than the fact that they were the innocent
instrument of drawing up a will. With the provisions of the
will they had nothing whatsoever to do, but you can explain
that till you are blue in the face if members of the family, or
relatives, feel that they have been unjustly treated. It is better
to leave wills alone.

As curate of the parish church with special oversight of the
Welsh congregation, my visiting area had been pointed out to
me — it included the business area of the town, and many
small streets housing a crowded population. It also included
the workhouse which was assigned to my charge and where I
was asked to make one visit a week, and to stick to the day
on which these visits had always been carried out. This was a
new world to me, a strange world, and a big world, for I
often got lost in its many wards and corridors, during my
first visits. Here had been swept the failures, the unfortunates
and the dregs of the Rhondda. Those who were not here were
in their graves or on beds in obscure corners and courts of the
valleys. It took me some time to get used to this world, and
to get over the feeling that I wished I hadn't to go there.
What helped me to get over it was the fact that I got to
know some of the inmates personally, loved to listen to their
reminiscences about men and places, and as much as anything
in that they knew it was my day and were expecting me and
would be disappointed if I did not turn up. I talked to
cripples, drunkards, the weak-minded, besides the genuine
unfortunates whom ill-health, business misfortunes, colliery
accidents, or a host of other things had thrown up here.

These were the lives which the Rhondda had broken and crushed, geared as it was from the first to the exploitation of its mineral wealth with little thought for the welfare of man. It saddened me, this workhouse; so far I had only seen and moved amongst healthy, strong men like myself, in college and in rural settings. However, it had now become my duty to visit the workhouse and I must not shirk that duty so early in my ministry. What also helped me, as I said, was the fact that some of the men, and the women too, whom I looked forward to having a chat with, and whom fate had given so many tumbles, but who had saved themselves from becoming sour and cynical, and in their despair curse everybody and everything, were expecting me. Two or three of the women impressed me as folks who ought to be given their discharge, and be allowed to try to build up their life once again, which they assured me was the one thing they desired.

Another of the inmates who also impressed me was a man of the name of Linus, a name of which he was obviously very proud, for one thing, of course, because it was borne by himself and by one other person at least, the first in a long list of distinguished personages who had filled the see of Rome — Linus, its first Bishop. Had Linus been the seventeenth Bishop, he would probably not have mentioned it, at any rate, as claiming any distinction, for what honour or distinction can be claimed by a person who only comes seventeenth in any effort, trial, competition or in a plain list of names. Distinction belongs to the man who is the first in any place, in any encounter; and also to the last — the man who stands, sword in hand, when all his comrades have fallen around him, standing to claim the victory in their name. But the seventeenth! Only a fool would claim that fame or honour belonged to being the seventeenth. Linus had been a schoolmaster and talked to me, not only 'learnedly', but also sensibly, and he seemed to me, like the two or three women, to deserve the chance to return to his profession, and lead a useful and honourable life once again.

What made my visits to the workhouse events to look forward to was the fact that there was a standing invitation to the visitor to have tea afterwards with the Master and the

Matron — Mr and Mrs Lewis: these good, kind people who with their children gave us such a warm welcome. This was one of those homes in the parish where the young clergy went often, and went when they missed their own homes, for a visit here was like a visit home, a place where one found understanding, concern and a liberty to do and say what young men of our age claim the privilege to indulge in.

To return to Linus: in his favour, I have already said he talked sensibly; he explained how circumstances had been against him and how misfortune had struck him. He spoke to me, as the women had, as one who trusted me and as one who was convinced that I could, if I only mentioned it to the right people, get him a chance to re-enter his profession once more, and in the service of its great ideals, regain his own personal dignity. I did not rush the matter, but I did not waste any time either. Here were at least three or four souls who only wished to get a little help to start life all over again. Of their ability and determination to make a success of it, they had not the slightest doubt, and I sincerely believed them, and from that day on was determined to press their case.

As I said, this invitation to tea on our visiting day was one of long standing. Mr and Mrs Lewis had known six or seven curates before me, and knew the pitfalls into which each one in his turn had fallen, and I can imagine Mr Lewis asking his wife: 'Has the young curate mentioned Linus yet?' to be told, 'No, not yet'. But it wouldn't be long now; all the curates had brought the same matters to their attention before; we had all to learn the same lesson. I remember very well the afternoon I mentioned it to Mrs Lewis. I can't say at this distance of time whether a faint smile played around her mouth. I do remember that she was so very nice about it, said she would mention it to the Master, and was glad that I was taking such a personal interest in the fate and future of the inmates. I felt that I was already beginning to do great things, of which this was only the start.

The following week the Master was at the table as well as the Matron and of course he brought up the matter I had broached to Mrs Lewis. Of Linus, he said he had had many chances, but back he came each time. He had had many jobs but had been unable to keep any of them, not from lack of ability, but because of the drink. That was his trouble. Poor Linus, he never went out again, and for the rest of his life he had only the possession of a great name to offer him whatever consolation it could. As for the women, they, too, had had their chances, but back they also came, bringing each a child with her. They would have fitted very well into this permissive, modern society, and with the aid of the 'Pill' would have remained respectable members of society. Looking back over this distance of time, I cannot help feeling sorry for them — they were women born before their time. My attempt to help them proved abortive, the only things that could help them were as yet fifty years in the future — modern aids and the more liberal modern thinking. I, of course, accepted the Master's explanation and opinion, but I was learning, and what a good job it was that I was beginning to learn early, for I had evidently such a lot to learn.

I think that Mr and Mrs Lewis would have been surprised, and would wonder what sort of parish priest I would make, if I had not been touched by the appeals of these unfortunate people, and had not been moved to try and help them. They would be happy to think that I was made of the right stuff at any rate, for they were good Christian people, and as it happened, members of our church.

THREE

Visiting

—————◦◦◦—————

OF MY VISITING, in general, I must say I liked it, and to be able to say that, means that I liked people, liked visiting them and liked talking to them. To be interested in people, to like people is an indispensable gift to a priest, for without it no ministry can be successful. Little is actually remembered after this lapse of time, but I know that I was welcomed in all homes, poor and rich alike. Where the Vicar had left a name out of the magazine, we, the curates, heard about it. Where the Vicar had really offended the family, our visit was made so much the warmer as a result — we could feel it, and soon realised that here we had to tread warily. I had to be specially so, for no Vicar could be popular with a congregation who were conscious that they only existed because it had been found possible to squeeze their service in between the normal services of the church. When that was not possible, they were allotted the church room. But on the whole I heard very little about it, they had by this time accepted their position as second-class members in their own church and in their own country. It must be remembered that they were loyal to their church — and to run down the Vicar or the church would be out of the question for a people who had been compelled to make such a hard choice, for there were plenty of strong Welsh chapels in the town to which they could go and have all the services in their own beloved language and enjoy first-class citizenship. But their church had come first. I have already mentioned that part of the town where the Vicar said he would be responsible for the visiting, but he would be surprised if he knew how often we, the curates, were in those homes, for here the parties were, and here the young people, with whom we felt so much at home, were — having just passed out of the student stage.

There were a few sick people on my visiting list. I have every reason to remember one in particular, for hers was the first sick visit I ever made: she was a young mother of about thirty-five with two small children, and she was far in the grip of consumption. To add to her suffering she knew she had an unfaithful husband who all the time was living and planning as if she were already dead. I had been given one or two tips about such visiting — one from my Vicar, not to stand between the door and the fire-place, or between the window and the fire-place, so as to be away from the germ-laden current of air carried between such places. I ought to explain here that I was a strong and healthy young man, having seen no serious sickness in my life up till now, for, all my life, I had mixed with healthy young men in school and college. I may add that during the fifty years my parents were at the farm, a visit from the Doctor was a very rare occurrence and never had a bier been brought to the door during that half-century. It was only natural I suppose, that I should therefore find infirm old-age, disease, sickness and deformity as something horrible and repulsive. In my visits to this young mother, I may have had visions of myself catching this dread disease and being myself in a matter of months, a wreck coughing up my life in a fevered and debilitated frame.

However, I felt I ought to carry out this simple and natural precaution given by my Vicar, and so took up my stand at the foot of the bed, well away from that current of air between the door and the fireplace. As I stood there I asked her how she was, and if there was anything that I could do for her. I did sincerely want my visits to be a comfort and a help to her. I can see her now, lying in bed, toothless, flushed, prematurely greying, haggard and lined, but in that wasting and decaying frame there ruled a will of steel, and a spirit that only death itself could crush — and that only after much wrestling. To my surprise I would find her sometimes downstairs doing the house-work and scrubbing the floor. She told me of her husband's unfaithfulness and the bitterness added fuel to the fire, the fever, that was already consuming her. Perhaps my visits did indeed bring her some comfort. I at any rate hoped so. But, no, I too, perhaps, wished her out of the way, so that these dreaded visits could end, for on my first or second visit as I stood there, at the foot of the bed, well away from that line between the fireplace and the door, she looked straight at me and asked 'Are you afraid?' That question stabbed me through the heart, I felt humiliated, found out to be a fraud and a hypocrite, pretending that I was happy in visiting her and offering her comfort and consolation. I was a failure. She could have said it differently, she could have considered my youth and my inexperience. But why should she? Here she was dying of consumption, suffering from weakness and pain, embittered by the knowledge that already another woman had taken her place in the affections of her husband, and before long would take her place in that very home and have the care of her children. In addition, here stood a young man who was afraid to come too near. Why should she consider my feelings or my age, so out it came: 'Are you afraid?' Few questions have stabbed me so deeply, but it had to come, I had to learn, and this was the way in which I was learning. And what a good thing it was that I was learning it at the commencement of my ministry. I never was afraid again, and no person during the whole of my ministry has ever had cause to ask that question again.

Looking back at that early experience over all these years, I realise now that my Vicar, or one of the curates, should have come with me on my first sick visits. I should have been told what to expect in a sick room and should have had an opportunity to watch, as a more experienced priest minis-tered comfort, consolation and cheer to a sick person — by touch, by word, by prayer and by sympathy.

In our last year in college the Principal took us in what was called *Parochialia:* a series of weekly lectures on how a well-organized parish was run, and of course a fully staffed parish as well, such, I suppose, as we had in St Catherine's, Pontypridd, where in a parish with a population of only eight and a half thousand, we had a Vicar, three curates, a Church Army sister and two Lay Readers. Will the church ever see such a staff — in proportion to the population — again?!

The Principal's lectures dealt mostly with parish organizations such as boys' and girls' clubs, C.E.M.S. and so forth. I do not remember that anything was said about visiting, but there could have been, though hardly anything about sick visiting. And even if there had, sick-visiting is something that can only be learnt in doing the actual work — in going round with an experienced priest, in watching him, and in listening to him; in fact, in serving an apprenticeship, after the manner of the old-time plumber or carpenter, going the rounds with the master and thus gradually learning the trade — or learn it in the rough-and-ready manner in which I was learning it.

Some old-fashioned bishops in the last century tried to help candidates for the ministry while they were in retreat for the Ordination. Archdeacon David Evans (St Asaph) tells us in his book *Adgofion Henafgwr* (The Reminiscences of an Old Man) how Bishop Vowler Short used to lie on the sofa at such times and pretend to be a sick person, and ask one of the candidates to pay him a sick visit. He adds that 'it is easier to imagine than to describe the feelings of the visitor'. Nevertheless, I suppose most clergy at some time or other in their life have wished for such an opportunity — some may even have prayed for it — to have their Bishop on the sofa before them and tell him what is wrong with him, and what he suffers from. And of course, as in all sick visits, offer up a prayer that he may be cured of it.

There was a gipsy encampment in the parish, under the arches of the railway. One day I was called to administer baptism in one the caravans where I found evidence of much preparation for my visit: the caravan was clean and tidy and everything that I needed was there already provided for me. Gipsies have peculiar ideas about baptism: they believe their children get on very much better after baptism. There were no unbaptised children in that encampment.

Though visiting took up most of my afternoons, one did have time to explore other parts of the Rhondda and the surrounding countryside, and visit college friends who like myself were getting used to their new world, for the Rhondda was full of curates in those days. I began early to devote all my mornings to reading and to study, until it soon became an established habit of life — indeed, I never had a spare moment but that I took up a book. The evenings were nearly all spent on some meeting or other of the young people, for we had all the clubs, societies, gatherings and organisations that were then deemed part of every well-worked and well-run parish. Amongst these, there was a men's guild, where very naturally I spent many evenings. In the course of the winter session we had debates, lectures, talks and there were cards, billiards, and the usual variety of games with which young people like to amuse themselves in the evenings. We had an annual summer trip; and in my first year, I remember, we went in an open waggonette drawn by two horses, to Southerndown, a stretch of coast that was beginning to become popular. On the way back we made many calls and as one of the curates was a good pianist we had a lot of singing. It wouldn't be a Welsh trip without singing.

The time came for me to receive my first pay for which I had worked and waited for three months — it was only four times a year the clergy were paid. Why that became the practice and why it is maintained must remain a mystery to most clergy, unless it is in the endeavour to keep our minds away from wages, from money; whereas weekly or monthly payments might bring it too often to our notice and render us a prey to its corrupting influences. I had naturally much looked forward to my first pay, it was a great day in my life; hitherto, and I was now twenty-three years of age, I had never earned a penny in my life. I took my cheque for £30 to the bank to cash it, and so received that number of golden sovereigns. Not many clergy alive today can say they drew their first pay in gold sovereigns, and not many either can boast that they went on a church trip in a waggonette. It is becoming obvious to readers that I belong to a very old world; quite true, but a happy old world, in every recollection of which I revel, though I would not like to live without the discoveries, advances, changes, and the sense of social security that now surrounds us.

The Rhondda of those days was throbbing with life; it is true it was war-time, but all the war had done so far was to step up a demand for many commodities, and in supplying this demand more men were needed. Those who said the war

would be over by Christmas were proved wrong; still a large
section of the community believed that it could not last
much longer. That was the prevailing mood in the Rhondda
for many months after I arrived there. The coal-mines were
working full out, the pubs were full, the shops were full, the
places of worship were full. Men had made money in the
Rhondda and were still making money. The place had faith in
itself and as far as anybody could see would go on
prospering. Coal was still the great motive power of the
world and there was no reason then to believe that it would
ever be supplanted. The vast majority of the people of the
Rhondda were miners, who, despite the grim surroundings of
their work and its heavy casualties, were a remarkably bright,
cheerful, friendly folk, gay and boisterous when they met in
any large numbers. Though the Rhondda itself was comparatively young, yet coal-mining was such an old occupation
in South Wales that a type had now been created: carefree,
friendly, music-loving, sport-loving, a type strong enough to
impress its image on every member. I remember many of my
age who had emigrated to the Rhondda from my home-
district. I met a large number of them there, and ten years
had been enough to complete the transformation from farm
servant to miner, sometimes much less. Yes, the Rhondda
was then a prosperous, happy, gay place — the blows, the
strikes, which shattered the Rhondda were more than a
decade away. I did not know the Rhondda of the Depression,
I was by then a parish priest out in the country, in
Radnorshire, but now and again a miner would call at the
door, asking for something to eat or somewhere to spend the
night as he scoured the country, looking for work. The
activity, the prosperity, the money, the gaiety had all gone.
These men were living images of the Rhondda that now was
— shattered, broken, begging, shy and ashamed, glad of a few
coppers and a kip in the straw. The song had died in their
heart, the lightness had gone out of the dragging feet. They
passed through Llandrindod Wells, a town that owed its
prosperity to the executives, the management and to the
more thrifty workmen of the iron, steel and coal industries of
South Wales, and as these men passed through they saw a
place dying with them, and dying of the same infectious

disease, for the malady could not be contained within the Rhondda or South Wales. For a South Walian to be able to say that he had taken his holiday at Llandrindod Wells, meant that he had arrived.

FOUR

Preaching:
The Welsh Way

OF MY PREACHING in those early days it behoves me to speak with great humility, though I know I did my best. As I composed my sermons I thought a lot of them, but as I read them over, which I did every day, I began to be less enthusiastic about them, until towards the end of the week, I was oftener than not utterly sick of them, and could see nothing in them at all. If I could deliver my sermons immediately I composed them, they would all, in my opinion, have been good sermons, but being of a somewhat nervous nature, I prepared as much of my work as I could well beforehand. I very often began to work on my sermon on Monday morning; indeed, I have known myself look up the collect for the following Sunday soon after I got home on Sunday evening. In the intervening days, I read my sermon over more than once a day so as not to be too closely tied to my manuscript, indeed, to be able, if possible, to preach it as if I had no manuscript at all; side-glances in that direction were intended to convey the impression that they were glances at the Bible, for I had always the Bible open in front of me, and placed in such a way as to hide my manuscript. Nobody ever saw that. I became such an adept at turning the pages — turning them so casually while I was looking into some corner of the church, that nobody could suspect what I was doing, or doing anything for that matter. I need hardly say, therefore, that when Sunday came I was thoroughly sick of my sermon and could see no good in it at all. Sometimes I got so ashamed of my effort that I began to write another. Now this feeling is known to all writers, not only to writers of sermons. Many have confessed that the enthusiasm which kept them going while they were writing, their growing pride in the inspired sentiments they were expressing, and expressing with such ease and richness of language, evaporates immediately the book is finished. While they were at it, they were kept going in the conviction that it was by far their best work and that it would indeed stun the world. If this sort of thing did not happen, and writers were not carried forward by the enthusiasm that the very act of writing generates, intoxicating them with grand notions of the value and the brilliance of what they were producing, very few books would have been written. This was the case with all my sermons, but I must say that in the case of one or two of them, my high opinion of them lasted until they were delivered. So, it has been rightly said that the author himself is not the best judge of his work, and authors have been warned not to be carried away by this feeling of disgust at the work they have just finished. It is a very natural reaction of the mind. It may be, therefore, that I am not the right person to talk about my sermons, for this peculiar reaction of the mind condemned them all except, as I said, in one or two cases. But as there is nobody else at this point of time to say anything about my early sermons, I have to continue with the task myself, and to continue, as I started, with all humility.

This I must say about my sermons: they were my best, and they were prepared with very great care. I never went into the pulpit not knowing what I was going to talk about, trusting   that inspiration would enable me to tackle any subject that the mind might suggest on the spur of the moment, as more than one had boasted to me they had done. One or two have even tried to justify their action by maintaining that one ought to allow more scope and rein to the Holy Spirit and let Him suggest the subject and the theme when one gets to the pulpit. I do not know whether the Holy Spirit works in that way, or only in that way. I can't see what advantage the Holy Spirit may see in delaying the suggestion of a subject to preach upon until one gets into the pulpit over suggesting it, and prompting one to study and meditation, on the previous Monday morning, or any other time during the week. How is it that so many get the impression that to have rules, to draw up plans, to make preparations, and to subject one's study and activity to a code of discipline, is to restrict to that extent the free access and guidance of the Spirit, that they are only a hindrance to his work and therefore can be one way of grieving Him? This attitude to one's work and duties may be agreeable to some type of person, but I have worked in the belief that rules, plans, preparations and the exercise of as much foresight as one is capable of, are as much in accord with the mind of the Holy Spirit as any other method. And because of this my sermons were always prepared early in the week.

Another thing about my sermons was that they were thoroughly evangelical and scriptural. I knew my Bible well — it had, in default of any other reading material for children, been my comic, my nursery rhyme and my fairy-tale book. There were in the vernacular at that time a few papers and magazines designed to meet the need of children, but none came our way, and never did I see one or hear of one from any of my school friends. As almost the exclusive pabulum for a child's mind, it was deficient on the comic side, but where stark violence was concerned it had more than enough to satisfy any child — that is, any boy. My early Bible-reading paid me valuable dividends in college and in my early sermon-making. To this may be added the ten years or so of Sunday School attendance which I had put in before I left home. When I think of those early sermons, they seem — as indeed they must have been — dull, commonplace and unexciting, and far from practical, for they took little note of the personal and social problems of people living in an industrial valley. However, my Vicar congratulated me on one of them: 'That was a good sermon'. They have all been long destroyed!

We were not given much help in college in composing or in the delivery of sermons. It is true we had in our final term in college to deliver a sermon of our own composition before one of the professors, who would then offer us criticism and advice, as our effort indicated how much of each we needed. I came off without much criticism as I had preached a sermon given me by the son of a neighbouring Vicar, who had been loaned three of his father's to choose from and as he needed only one, he offered me my choice of the other two. I got good marks for it, and I made use of it in my early curacies. Those of us who were Welsh-speaking had the added advantage of going to one of the surrounding mission churches, accompanied by the professor of Welsh, who on our journey back offered us kindly advice and encouragement. It is true that at our Deacon's examination we were given a list of sermons preached by the leading Anglican preachers, amongst them, the sermons of Liddon and Robertson. The trouble with these, more particularly with Liddon's, was that they were too long, and already slightly antiquated. A fellow curate of mine timed one of Liddon's sermons and found that it took him an hour and twenty minutes to read through at a good reading pace. There was a way however of using such a sermon, even as late as the early 'twenties, for I was told of a certain Lay Reader whose sermons mystified his congregation. They said he would start off most brilliantly and they felt they were going to get something worth listening to that day, for he was clearly leading them forward to a dissertation on, and an exposition of a great spiritual truth, only to have it all, greatly to their disappointment, abruptly terminated, leaving them as it were hanging in mid-air. The next time he came, he started in mid-air and discoursed away up there in the clouds, very brilliantly, they said, illuminating with rhetorical sweeps some great truth which they wished they knew what it was, but before they could discover, or guess, what it was, there was another abrupt ending, leaving them as they were found — hanging in mid-air.

On the third occasion, again starting in mid-air, the congregation felt that he was putting the roof on a house that wasn't there, that hadn't been built, a beautiful roof, of course, if only it had walls to rest on. However, they were treated to a fine climactic peroration, and that was all. In the end it was found out what was happening: he was in the habit of taking one of Liddon's sermons and breaking it up into three. Did he visit the same mission church on successive Sundays while he was on that particular sermon, the congregation might have greatly benefitted, but as a month, or even two months, could intervene between his visits, mystification and disappointment was the only result.

I never did that. I never, for years, made use of any other man's sermon in the mistaken and foolish notion — and fear — that other churchpeople read what I read, and when I ventured to incorporate a sentence or a paragraph from an outside source, however obscure, I quaked as I read it in case somebody in the congregation stood up and pointing an accusing finger at me, shouted: 'Hi, stop, you've cribbed that. It is obvious now that you don't make your own sermons, you buy them. We can do that. We don't pay you to read to us other people's sermons'. It was very foolish of me, of course, and it shows how much — how very much — I had to learn. And yet one of the tips I had been given, and that by a nonconformist minister, who used to come and visit us occasionally — and who was always very cordially welcomed as a respected neighbour — was never to be afraid to make use of other people's works. In time — but it took some time — I became brave enough to act literally on his advice, as growing experience convinced me that the average church-member reads no church paper, and certainly no books of sermons.

Nevertheless the working man holds in contempt the clergyman, however good a preacher he is, who does not compose his own sermons, and it was in this attitude and atmosphere I was brought up. The author of *Richard Wilton — A Forgotten Victorian* says that when he became Vicar of Kirby Wharfe he received 'a deputation who solemnly enquired if he wrote his own sermons, for some said they were copied from a book. But Richard, to prove that his sermons were his own, offered to preach the following Sunday on any test they chose to give him'.

One of the curates had enough sermons to last him, he told me, three years; and when he came to the last, he just turned the pile over and started once again with the first. I was aghast. Had he no respect for himself. People must surely know them off by heart — and could he go up to the pulpit Sunday after Sunday and preach old sermons, utterly insensitive to the danger of being accused of preaching old sermons. Such a foolhardy practice was incomprehensible to me. On this matter again I have changed my mind. Where sermons are concerned, congregations have very short memories — the duration reflecting the attention they paid to them when they were delivered. In my own case — and I am sure this is the experience of a large number of clergy — when going over an old stock of sermons, I could swear, of many of them, that I never wrote them and never preached them, so completely had they gone out of my mind. We can well believe therefore that a member of the congregation who had given the semon just the usual, polite attention — out of his respect for his Vicar — could sincerely swear in two years' time — often in a much shorter period — that he had never heard it in his life before, provided the preacher had used no striking illustration in it, or illustrated it with a story, the humour or pathos of which had caught his imagination. So those who like to preach old sermons may do so without any fear of detection — but — in every congregation there are one or two to whom sermons mean so much; they seem to live for sermons and if they happen to be present, the preacher has had it. As it is possible that these memoirs of mine may be read by a few clergy, it is not necessary for me to tell them of the many ways there are of rigging up an old sermon in a new dress, beginning with the text, which here may be regarded as the hat, a very important article in any attempt at disguise.

Poor as my early efforts probably were, I must confess that I tried to preach good sermons, and to be a good preacher — yes, even a great preacher. How could it be otherwise in a country which looked up to, and which gave such respect and honour to the great and popular preacher. They moved like princes amongst our people, and were received almost on bended knee, such was the universal reverence with which they were regarded. I should be less than human if I did not covet the acclaim and homage of my people. Though to shine as a master of the art of preaching may at this early stage have been present in my mind as a wish and a hope, certainly not as a well-formed ambition, yet I could not descend to using arts and practices that were attributed, and I believe rightly, to some of my contemporaries: for example, the practising of the most effective manual acts, postures and gestures before a mirror, and the trying out of artificial pauses merely for the sake of effect. It is true that I have looked at myself in the mirror in the act of speaking and preaching, but some shame always came over me. I felt I was playing with my true and honest self. It was all so unnatural and conceited to strive there after the mere outward effect of postures, pauses and gestures, which should come only as the natural result of the earnestness and the urgency with which the message was being delivered. I had at all times to be true to myself; any artificial or acquired pose or manner in the pulpit has always been anathema to me. Never have I been able to get into that homely, intimate pose of leaning on the pulpit rail to wag a finger at the congregation, nor again to thump the Bible, or take it up and strike the pulpit desk with it, producing artificial claps of thunder. And this reminds me of what I was told by a nonconformist deacon, that in his home church when he was a boy they would never put the best Bible on the pulpit when a particular minister visited the chapel, for he was notorious for the violence with which he handled it. An old one was specially kept for the purpose. I had as I said to be true to myself — I have a fairly tall and erect figure, and I have always stood up in the pulpit exactly in the attitude in which I would face anybody who wished to speak to me, deeming that to be correct and sufficient, exhibiting that diffidence and humility which should never be absent in one privileged to speak in the name, and in the place, of his Redeemer. I have seen in the Welsh pulpit eyes that flash defiance and visages contorted into a snarling, spitting ferocity, equalled only by a caged and savage beast, as they work themselves up into a pitch of fervency, in which only they deem it possible for the gospel message to be delivered.

Now we of the Church in Wales did not think it necessary to take such heavy pieces of artillery into the pulpit, though we had our big guns, and could call them up as the occasion demanded. But normally the usual Sunday sermon was delivered in our churches without raising one's voice, and certainly without shouting, which was invariably expected in the nonconformist pulpit, that is, the firing of the artillery pieces.

I have said that I prepared my sermons with great care. I

have also said that I wanted to be a good preacher, even a
great preacher. I was brought up in a land, and in an age, of
great preaching. There were amongst us masters of assemblies
who could stir, thrill and electrify the masses who listened in
awed silence to the lashing fury of the rhetorical hurricane
that carried them with it. Had not John Elias turned a fair,
notorious for its evil fame and excesses, into a preaching
session, and does not the good book tell us that St Peter
preached with such power and unction on the day of
Pentecost that three thousand were added to the church that
one day. Oh, yes, I certainly believed in the power of
preaching. It would be terrible to think that any young man
began his ministry without holding to that as one of the
profoundest of his convictions. And thereby hangs a tale. I
did want very much to preach a sermon on that early
experiment of the church in Christian social sharing — its
determination to accept responsibility for the personal
welfare and security of all the members of its rapidly growing
movement. We read that 'all that believed . . . . . had all
things in common', that all who were 'possessors of lands or
houses sold them and brought the prices of the things that
were sold and laid them down at the apostles' feet, and . . .
Barnabas . . . having land, sold it, and brought the money and
laid it at the apostles' feet'.

That early experiment of the church always appealed to
me and I felt very strongly that I would like to commend it
again to the church of the twentieth century.

It is rare for us to be told what result followed the
preaching of any particular sermon. If a reporter were present
at Brighton when Robertson was preaching, or at St Paul's
when Canon Liddon was preaching, he might, as I am sure he
could, just round off his report by saying that the congregation filed out of church in a quiet and orderly manner. But
it was very different back in Jerusalem at the Feast of
Pentecost. St Luke describes the mighty results of that early
apostolic preaching, and a man might well be appalled at the
thought — the possibility — of its happening again, and the
stoutest heart would hesitate as he contemplated what the
sudden access of three thousand new members would entail.
It would mean the acquiring of a new site and the building of

a new church to accommodate them. Some successes can produce as many problems as disasters.

I read these verses over again — read how the people sold their land and their houses and brought the money 'and laid it at the apostles' feet'. What if my hearers were moved to do the same, sell their houses, break up their homes, bring the proceeds — and their children — to me and leave them in my care, asking only to be directed to Africa, or some other heathen country, to help spread the Christian gospel! I couldn't allow this sort of thing to happen. I could not preach that sermon.

I have just said what a tragic thing it would be for a young priest to start his ministry, doubting the power of preaching. That would be bad enough, but to start one's ministry by refusing to preach on a certain text, or subject, or on any article or question, vital to the faith and mission of the church, because of the consequences — because someone or some section, might be offended, would be more tragic still. So I preached my semon and the result can be given in two words: nothing happened. Or as our imaginary reporter might say, the congregation filed out of church in a quiet and orderly manner. No title-deed was handed to me, no child was left in my care. It was obvious I was no St Peter. I had not been present in that upper room when ' . . . . . tongues, like as of fire' came down.

Of course, I was young and had a lot to learn, but despite everything I never lost faith in the power of preaching, so much did this faith and assurance remain with me throughout my ministry that I always prepared my sermons with the utmost care. To confirm me in my faith, there came to my notice, sometimes through my reading, sometimes through the testimony of some individual, the heartening example of how instances of apostolic preaching still produced Pentecostal results. In a later curacy, I was told of a working man who brought out his life's savings (£74) and put them on the collection plate in response to his Vicar's fervent appeal on behalf of the missionary work of the church. I count it as one of the privileges of my life to have know him personally.

I learnt early that congregations do not like jokes in the pulpit, nor slang and certainly not the use of swear words, even in quotations. A humorous situation or a comic turn of events is always secretly enjoyed even though one cannot of course give adequate expression to one's enjoyment in church. These can happen at any time in any service. I remember once taking a wedding — and I ought to say here that I always spoke very clearly and very deliberately in those parts where the young couple had to repeat the words after me, for they are largely unfamiliar to them — when I said: 'With this ring I thee wed', the way I heard it repeated was: 'With this thing I thee wed'.

There are different ways of ending a sermon; I don't like the snap ending favoured by some, where, without any warning at all, the preacher suddenly stops as if he has just remembered something he should have attended to. I prefer ways that transmit a hint or a sign to the congregation that the end is nor far off, such as was followed by an old Anglesey Vicar: when the congregation saw his hands moving under his surplice and his fingers working away, they knew he was coming to the end — he was filling his pipe!

There was in the Welsh pulpit a manner of preaching unknown to the rest of christendom. It was of a musical character, akin in its quieter moods to the melodies and refrains of Gregorian chanting — and called THE HWYL. As I have described it in my *My Own Folk* I will say no more about it here.

The old Welsh clergy out in rural Wales who knew their parishes and their families so well, had an easy, familiar and intimate way with them in the pulpit. They would often refer to a member of the congregation by name, and the services were not allowed to become too stiff, and cold and mechanical, with a mechanical parson in the pulpit talking to a static congregation. The following incident will illustrate it — it was told me by my father, as an old man, for we had been talking about the ways of the old clergy and in particular about the Reverend John Williams, our own Vicar at one time, who had earned the name of *Y tafod aur* (the golden tongue) for his attractive and impressive eloquence in the pulpit. The occasion was that of a christening, and my father had harnessed the mare and brought my mother, the baby and the few friends and neighbours in the farm gambo, an act of consideration which won at once the approval and admiration of his Vicar. Later on, in the sermon he called attention to it: 'Now, Tom, this morning, has set you all a good example, he has brought his gambo to carry the mother and child and her friends to church. Too many of you allow the mother to come on her own and to carry the baby all the way. Now Tom has set you this morning a good example: in future come with the mother to the baptism, and bring the gambo to carry her and the child in comfort'. As I said, he was an old man when he told it me, and it was obvious that he recalled that early day with some pride because of the pleasure it had then given him — to be given a special mention by his own Vicar and to be held up before his fellow-parishioners as one who, though young, had given them a good example. And why not? Ordinarily, what he heard from the pulpit was some good advice, or good example one of the apostles or one of the patriarchs of the Old Testament had given; then one day it became his own turn to be mentioned in the company of these great men. It was a proud moment. Did he feel — just for that moment — that he had acquired apostolic stature! The story ended in a sort of anticlimax, for my mother, (we had almost forgotten her) he said, did not like it at all. She was a shy and reserved person, and though my father was a kind and considerate man — as this act proves — she must know in her heart of hearts that he was far from reaching the stature of an apostle. This is one example of the closeness and the intimacy of the relationship which existed between priest and people — and why should it be different on Sunday from any other day!

That reminds me of what I was told by the granddaughter of one of my predecessors — The Rev. Arthur Griffiths (1850–1900). He had a famous brother, an Archdeacon, and a very considerable figure in Eisteddfodic circles. It was only natural therefore that he should make use of him for special occasions, such as harvest festivals. As the lady decorators had hung bunches of grapes round the pulpit, he picked a grape when he felt he needed one, and munched away. What he did with the pips I was not told, but a man who can preach a sermon and at the same chew a grape would not be greatly incommoded by a problem of that sort. Before we condemn him, or throw even a grape stone at him, let us remember that in those days he would be expected to preach for at least an hour.

Soon after my arrival at Pontypridd, the Anglican church began to organise that very fine effort of the First World War, the *National Mission of Hope and Repentance.* As my Vicar was the Diocesan secretary, I, as his own personal curate, having not the charge of a particular mission church and a district, apart from the care of the Welsh congregation, was called upon to do a great deal of the 'office' work to help him. We addressed innumerable envelopes and enclosed endless circulars. Without attempting to tell its story as it functioned and ran its course in the diocese of Llandaff, I can say it was one of the finest and sincerest efforts of the Anglican church — and it did a lot of good. Possibly the results were not in all places commensurate with the vast effort made, nevertheless, and I will say it again, it was a fine and sustained effort. Along with all the other bodies, sections, departments and services which were working all-out for the survival of the nation, the church was there, too, doing its very utmost to uphold the morale of the people and to strengthen its faith, giving it the assurance, that with humility and repentance in our hearts, the just God would give us the victory. Yes, the church could be heard at work, and seen at work; like the munition workers, the farming community, the merchant navy, the church, too, was at it. I have lived long enough to hear it spoken lightly of, but as one who can speak with personal knowledge of that period and that effort of our church, I can truly say that it was one of the finest and sincerest efforts the church was ever engaged in.

The *office* part of the campaign in the Vicarage study brought me and my Vicar very much closer together. As we were there for hours together and as the work demanded very little concentration, the mind was left free to wander at will all over the world and dwell on scenes and dramas of personal involvement and achievement. Amongst other things I learnt that he was a crack shot, and it is very remarkable how mastery and superiority in certain athletic and sporting fields win our admiration rather than many of the others which require very much longer training and a higher degree of skill. Why should we immediately feel admiration for, and feel envious of, the fellow who has a reputation for being a crack shot, a hard rider to hounds, or good with his fists? I fancy that in the case of the first two it has something to do with the aura that surrounds the gun and the horse — that's why the sharp-shooter and the rider have been so widely exploited in novel and film.

When, gradually, I became familiar with the clergy and saw their life from the inside, I must confess I had a few mild shocks. I knew clergy smoked and took a glass of beer and I had heard of some who took too many. I had never seen a clergyman drunk of course, but I did see one later on, towards the end of my curacy in Pontypridd. It was a young curate coming home from a church trip either to Ilfracombe or Weston: two or three laymen were holding him up, having, for the sake of the cloth, divested him of his clerical collar and his hat. The tales in circulation about clerical topers were generally reminiscences, and had reference to the clergy of a previous generation who, I can proudly say, had by my time been replaced by a more conscientious, sincere and hard-working lot of men.

But to see clergy doing very ordinary jobs somewhat jarred — to see a parish priest whitewashing the scullery, cleaning out under the calves, or driving two or three bullocks to the mart (fairs in those days). It was possibly all due to my inexperience and the natural reaction of one who had been brought up to look upon the clergy as an order apart, and certainly above doing what is normally done by farm workers. I was, undoubtedly, in my Ordination year prepared to make a more definite break with the world and its ways, its demands and its values. Of course, I was young and had a lot to learn and one of the things I had to learn, or rather to be reminded of, was that the mission of our Redeemer was to the world and not to the church, and that if we were to have a part in that mission we had to get closer to the world, and more deeply involved in all its problems and struggles.

But to return to my early mild shocks, I had to learn that clergy were after all only human. If I did not know it before, such a scene as the following could not fail to bring it home to me. Scene: the Vicarage study, *dramatis personae:* Vicar and his young curate — the study window overlooks the drive. Vicar: 'Who are these two women coming up the drive? What the heck do you think they want? I know, they've come to apply for that vacant post in the day-school. Go and tell them I am not in. No. Wait. They are the fourth party to come this week. I shall be glad when the blasted post is filled. I am sick and tired of the whole bloomin' business'. Laymen, I knew, spoke like this, and used swear words, but I never thought clergy 'let go' in this fashion. It had to be borne in on me sometime that clergy after all were only human, and such a scene could only have been sent to impress the fact upon me. Such an explosion was possibly the best thing that could have happened at that moment, for it provided a vent for the relief and release of pent-up feeling. One has to let off steam sometimes to prevent a burst. Once the explosion was over, the chief actor in this little drama became quite calm, and by the time the two women were shown in to the study was even gracious to them. It couldn't have been anything but a good thing.

Another shock came when older clergy, oblivious of my presence and of any effect it might have on my mind, discussed openly amongst themselves the shortcomings of their bishops, and their complete lack of those gifts and qualities so essential to the proper exercise of that exalted office. 'How ever he became a bishop, heaven only knows, and fancy making Jack Evans a canon, "Jack the sweets" as we used to call him. It just shows he doesn't know his clergy'. (Jack Evans, now a canon, got his name because his mother kept a little shop in the village, which sold, mostly, sweets.) To me at that time to speak thus of superiors — and much more in the same strain — bordered almost on blasphemy. Why, all clergy were to me an order apart, much more so the bishops, these venerable figures who flitted on rare occasions from one crowded church to another, robed in vestments that again suggested that they were a race apart. Even more so did their week-day wear emphasise it, for if there was anything made, or worn, calculated to call attention to itself, as being odd, awkward, bizarre and unpractical, this was it.

Nothing that was ordinary distinguished them at any time. Twice only in my life before had I come into contact with a bishop, and each time I was on my knees — at my Confirmation and Ordination. Later on in life, when I heard a clergyman say that if his bishop applied for a junior curacy he was at the time advertising, he would not consider him for one moment. I thought the ultimate had been heard of in dispraise of bishops. Thus dethroned, this venerable order of beings whom I had previously regarded as inhabiting a region somewhere in the clouds, indeed above the clouds, were brought down to earth, and here they stood in front of me in all their human nakedness, having been, as it were, by the verdict of their contemporaries, deprived and unfrocked. After getting over the first shock, and viewing them at close quarters on my own human level, I must confess I much preferred them this way. They looked not only human but quite ordinary and undistinguished; some not even ashamed of the nicknames they acquired in school or college days, not over-anxious to hide one or two likeable human weaknesses. And did I have a vacant curacy at the time, unlike my colleague, I think I would consider very favourably the application of one or two of them. Anyhow, I liked them in their new look, and I never put them back in the sky again, for I felt I should be doing them a great wrong.

FIVE

Across Offa's Dyke:
Diocese of Chester

———⊃⊂———

WHEN MY TWO YEARS were nearly up in Pontypridd, I began
to look round for fresh fields and pastures new. I say two
years, for at that time it was felt to be the right and proper
thing to give your Vicar at least one year as a priest. He had
given you your title and had put up with you as a deacon,
when you could only be used as it were in second gear.
Having done that, and a little more, I felt I was now justified
in seeking another curacy, and, if possible, in a still bigger
parish, for I was anxious while I was young to get as varied
and as extensive an experience as I could. I was conscious all
the time that my world — a rural community upbringing, a
Grammar School education in the next parish and a college
education in the next county — was a very small one. I had
already got out into a considerably bigger world, that of the
Rhondda, but there was a bigger world than even the
Rhondda, and it was calling. So I followed carefully the
advertisement columns of the *Church Times*, and eventually
found one that I thought would suit me. I did not know the
place, but I looked up the map and found that it was not far
from Manchester, and concluded naturally that it was in the
diocese of Manchester, but later found that it was in the
diocese of Chester — STOCKPORT. However, it was near
enough to Manchester, and it partook entirely of the
character of a Lancashire town, except that its industries
were more varied than that of a purely cotton town. But
before looking out for anything in this country, I had
seriously thought of joining the Bush Brotherhood in
Australia. It appealed to me immensely, partly — or largely —

because one was given a horse, and I could imagine myself riding over vast tracts of the Bush, reading, even making my sermons on horseback. Readers of my first book will remember my early attachment to the horse.

In Stockport, in a parish of fourteen thousand (St Thomas's) I certainly had new experiences. To start with, the people were different. I was now for the first time amongst English people. I had, of course, known intimately a few English people before, some I palled up with in school and college. On my advent to the parish my Vicar took me round that part which would be in my special care. He pointed out certain streets and landmarks, mostly chimney stacks, and said: 'this will be your district and special responsibility'. I said to myself, this is all right, it won't take me long to cover this — I had of course visiting in mind. The ground area of my new district seemed to me to be the size of one of our fields at home — and it was, I suppose, very natural that one brought up on a farm should make such comparisons. But I was mistaken. They say a Welsh mile becomes longer as you walk it, so does the crowded area of a cotton town become bigger as you begin to work it. As big fleas have little fleas upon their backs, so long streets have little streets upon their backs, besides innumerable odd courts and alleys, which swarm with human beings, especially with children. Some of these streets hidden behind others had only one lavatory for the use of all the families. The older parts of my district were just slum areas; anyhow, such a vast area of teeming humanity I had never seen before, nor imagined possible, so when I got to know it in some detail, I had to add another of our fields — and of a similar acreage — to it.

I found the English people of course different from Welsh people. They appeared more forthright and outspoken in their conversation — more definite and emphatic in their opinions and statements. I mean, of course, the North-country working man, such as made up the population of the parish. We, the Welsh, are much quieter people, more reserved and less voluble. It would indeed be strange if these teeming thousands within a radius of ten miles of Manchester — that human bee-hive — were not alert and on their toes, for life was highly competitive. The man who wanted to get on —

or even to keep from slipping back — had to be at it for all he
was worth; he dared not allow himself to slacken for one
moment. Living, here, involved a much fiercer struggle than I
had ever known, or ever imagined life could be. Men could
not afford to waste time with niceties of words, or
refinement of conduct. And every man was what he was by
his own unaided efforts — his parents would not have been
able to help him, except in the example they had given him
of diligence, pluck and determination. A man was what he
was for what had happened in his own lifetime. Most were
self-made men. Now, we in Wales, on the other hand, were
what we were because of what had happened in the last
hundred or two hundred years. Changes rarely took place in
the fate and fortune of families, or individual members of
families, in the course of two or three hundred years. A
family was proud to say that it had lived on that farm for so
many generations. Things move slowly in the country, tied to
the progress of the seasons. In such a calm and orderly
progress, there was no room for aggressiveness or competition, only for patience and co-operation, for nature refused
to be forced. In haymaking time and harvest time, there
might be an occasional race with the weather. As pressure
from no quarter was placed upon us, we could keep open
minds on a lot of questions; seldom were we forced to make
sudden decisions or form definite opinions. But, here, I
found a people uneasy in themselves if they had not definite
opinions and made-up minds, with the result that they were
quite prepared to make them up upon the strength of one
article in an evening paper.

A man with a very definite opinion is in the nature of
things prepared always to express it — however acquired —
even, as I said, from an article in an evening paper. Anyhow,
you know where you are with such people, for they are
forthright, and express their minds boldly and clearly. Now
we country people do not feel that we have to have an
opinion on every question, problem and mystery in the
universe, and even if we do hold opinions on a lot of things,
we don't feel that we have to make them known to
everybody.

Thinking back, perhaps the difference that I noticed on

first acquaintance, was not so much the difference between Welsh and English as between country people and town people. As the country produces a certain type of person, so does the pulsating, industrial town, and we must learn to understand each other, without attributing to the other person motives less generous than we are prepared to apply to ourselves.

The newness of the situation and the strangeness of my field of work, in addition to the differences that I noticed in the people, were striking me with double force, for in addition to being a countryman, I was also a Welshman. However, I was up there in my new sphere of work because I had a very definite opinion and a set purpose, which was to get to know more of the big world outside than it had been my lot as a country lad to know, and to learn how the church was responding to the problems and demands made upon it by such conditions as were immediately obvious to a newcomer: bad housing, overcrowding, poverty and the resultant crop of evil and misery.

After the initial impressions of strangeness and newness began to wear off, I soon became blended into the new society, even acquired, I think, a little more push and drive myself, for one could not be unaffected by the quality of the life around him.

I certainly got to like them — plain, honest, hard-working people, outspoken, with other and deeper qualities about them than one would suspect on the first impact. As proof of what I have said, I may here state — but more of that later — that I felt I would like to live with one of them for the rest of my life, and so it came about that when the war was over, we were married, and never was a man more abundantly blessed in a partnership and a companionship that lasted fifty years to within a few months. And I am prepared to argue now that deep down, when we get to know one another well, there is very little difference between the Welsh and the English. The reader will note that I said 'very little difference', and just that little difference persisted along the years, just enough to add spice to a common domestic fare that might otherwise become stale and insipid.

I had new and wider experiences in England than I could

have had in Wales; not that the work in itself was different, though there was much more of it — more visiting, more evenings out with some organisation or other, more functions, more workhouse visiting and more funerals. As there was a troop of Scouts belonging to the church, I became a Scout.

I have already mentioned some of the things that struck me on first impact as being different, one of which was the readiness and the forthrightness with which the people aired their views and spoke their minds.

Another thing that struck me was the number of people that were suffering from various kinds and various degrees of deformity, amongst them the knock-kneed, the bow-legged, the hunchback and the cripple. I had never noticed anything like that in Pontypridd, though very naturally quite a number showed evidence of colliery accidents, but no noticeable number bearing congenital disabilities. They might make up only a very small proportion of a population, considerably larger than that of Pontypridd. Nevertheless, they were numerous enough for me to become aware of their existence. I knew something of the history of the cotton towns of the North and the rise of the industrial era. These were now the third and fourth generation that were paying the price of the greed and the inhumanity of the masters who employed child labour in their mills. When I recalled the early years of the industry, the long hours, the low wages, the bad housing conditions, my surprise was not that they were so many, but that they were so few.

One such young girl I used to visit regularly, a cripple, whose legs were supported by irons and straps — she took in contract work from Christy's hat works in the town, and all day long her fingers moved like lightning, so rapid that one could hardly follow them. If men will look inside their hats, they will see at the back a small light bow — she tied twelve dozen of these (144) for threepence!

I had another surprise: On the first Whit Monday morning, I found the main street of the town — Buxton Road — black with people making for the plains of Cheshire or the hills of Derbyshire. Houses, factories and streets were already beginning to hem them in and moving the green fields and leafy lanes farther and farther away from them so that it was only during the public holidays that they could enjoy them. Anyhow, here they were striding out valiantly, in groups of two or three, up to groups that could be a Sunday school class or the membership of a club or pub. This not only surprised me, I felt it also challenged me: Here was I, a countryman, who had never bothered about it at all — so much of it was always there that one took it for granted. Even in the Rhondda one was not far from the countryside, a stiff walk up the hills and lo! the whole of the industrial valleys were folded up in their deep and narrow beds, and out of sight. Presented with this challenge, I, too, began to strike out into the country — town folk were not going to beat me in my native element, and this brought me memorable journeys, often, in the company of the schoolmaster (Mr Catlow) up to the hills and vales of Derbyshire and the plains of Cheshire. I remember some of the villages still: Kinder Scout, New Mills, Mottram in Longdendale, Disley, Lyme Handley, Werneth Low.

Stockport was a two-storey town. The ground floor was built along the river on which you looked down from the upper part, as it were from upstairs. Weaving began as a domestic industry in these parts, and the high three-storey houses are evidence of the extent to which it was carried on in the homes: and when it got out of the home, it did not move very far away so that one is left with the novel sight of mills and stacks jostling for space with the streets, courts and alleys around them.

My fellow curate was another Welshman, the Rev. John Arnold Pruen James, son of Mr Ifor James (1840-1909), the first Registrar of the University of Wales, who, I learnt later, was a distinguished figure in a small coterie of Welshmen who were then working hard to establish a university for the Principality. He was also a knowledgeable man in many periods of Welsh history, but he is best known for the small volume he wrote — published in 1890 — under the title of 'The Source of the Ancient Mariner' (of Coleridge) to prove that the hero of that story was a Captain Thomas James, (see D.N.B.) Well, my colleague it was who in a big way introduced me to the study of modern psychology. I had not as yet had much time, since my examinations were over, to look very carefully at the many fields of study that were open to me. So far I had been learning my first job, involving myself with people — people of all ages, in Sunday School and junior organisations, in adult classes and societies, and of course in pastoral work within the membership of the church, and outside amongst the lapsed and unattached. My colleague was also in charge of a mission church in a district with slightly worse housing conditions than mine.

In these crowded and squalid streets I never met a Welshman, and hardly ever a Scotsman; for the most part, the population was made up of Irish families and the improvident native English. There were Welshmen in Stockport as one will find in any sizeable town in England, but they were for the most part, chemists, teachers, shop-keepers or shop-assistants, builders, doctors and of course clergy and ministers. And they all seemed to be doing well for themselves. In these crowded and poorer streets of the town one would come across a neatly kept, clean house, inhabited perhaps by an old couple, or by a family who all these years had kept themselves securely above and beyond all the pressures and all the influences that had made the slums. In nearly all cases the power that had kept them and their families from being swamped by the menacing tide was the power of religion. I was pointed out streets that within the memory of those who told me were once respectable streets where the decent families of the town lived. Generally, the first step in the story of its deterioration was the letting of one house to a feckless family of low character. What happened next was that the respectable people next door, as soon as they could get a suitable house, moved out and the only tenant the landlord could now get was another of the character of the people he had allowed to come in in the first place. In a very short time the desert had gained another plot of ground as the decent people, generally for the sake of their children, had abandoned it to them, and the transformation was complete — another slum street had been made.

I am talking now of the second decade of this century, and of the housing and the conditions that then prevailed, when hardly any legislation had been passed to protect tenants and to compel landlords to keep to some standard of repair and decency the properties for which they charged rents.

Misfortune drove many into these poor and squalid quarters. I once came across a man who had evidently come down in the world, and apparently had philosophically accepted his new world and married a woman of the working class. Here, at any rate he had been lucky, for she was a good, patient soul who kept a clean house for him and who tended to his needs with care and devotion. He had been educated in a public school, and would sometimes regale me with recitations from Virgil, the unparalysed arm held ecstatically above his head — he was now bed-ridden — as he entered into the spirit of the passage, revelling for the moment perhaps in memories of happier days in the classroom and the more opulent surroundings. The recitations ceased, for we had offended him. He suspected that we were supplying him with free milk, and public school men do not accept free milk: they will accept poverty, but not charity!

If misfortune drove some people into the slums, ownership kept others there: Once, the street was quite respectable, and substantial people lived there, owning their own house, possibly three or four houses. As the character of the street and the district deteriorated, so the majority of the tenants moved away, but occasionally it was discovered that one family had remained, represented now perhaps by two maiden sisters, who, out of love for the old home and out of sentiment for a property that their parents and grandparents thought such a lot of, refused to leave. In a house more pretentious than the others, these refined ladies would keep up habits and a way of life that, since it all contrasted so markedly with the present surroundings, seemed so much more charming and attractive. Such people could be a great influence for good in these districts. Known to belong to a previous and more respectable level of existence, they were naturally looked up to and respected, as being ladies, and ladies not at all ashamed of living amongst them. Problems were referred to them, and their advice often respected. They certainly were of great help to the church and the clergy, as they could acquaint them of any cases of sickness or distress. Frequently such folk were Sunday school teachers and thus

were able to get many families to send their children to
Sunday school, often adding little attractions and rewards of
their own. Young mothers who had been in service with them
were regular visitors and were welcomed and advised with
motherly concern and affection. Yes, such women — referred
to generally as 'the ladies' — who had graciously, uncomplain-
ingly accepted the change that came over the area could lead
very full, very useful and very happy lives.

I like these older, neglected, and poorer parts of old towns;
one never knows what one will come across in them. Here,
old craftsmen, employed in the decaying crafts of an older
world, still ply their skill, having plenty of customers who
value good workmanship, turned out by men who are masters
of their trades. Here, too, survive some of the humbler crafts
— that of the tinsmith, the basket maker, the watch repairer
and the druggist — possibly in premises bearing the fading
legend: 'Established 1792'. Here is a dark, low bookshop.
Not far away, with two or three fishing rods in the window,
lives the man who makes fishing flies and other tackle for
anglers like his father and grandfather before him, and who
can tell you what fly to use for what river, for what weather
and for what month of the year. There was, and there still is
a great deal of commerce between the better parts of our old
towns and the darker, meaner streets, generally to be found
in that area round the ancient parish church. To one such
house in an obscure street, a friend took me where lived an
old lady who made shirts. One took one's own material to
her and she made them up for, if I remember rightly,
eighteen pence.

I don't know that in this, my second curacy, I introduced
any new manner or method into my preaching. All young
curates try to become less and less tied to their manuscripts
and reach forward to a new, freer and more intimate
relationship between pulpit and pew, but hesitate to make
changes in case they are noticed, smiled at, or indeed adverseley
commented upon: 'What is coming over our new curate
lately, he used to be quiet enough, but he has now begun to
throw his arms about, lean over the pulpit and thump the
Bible. I think he is getting too big for his boots and is trying
to imitate that pulpit giant, John Jones Llanfawr'. Congreg-

ations do not like to see changes and experiments carried out in the pulpit before their very eyes. So, nearly all curates, after they've given their Vicar a full year's service as a priest, begin looking for another curacy, and another pulpit. As for myself, though it was my endeavour all the time to rely less and less on my manuscript, it was with considerable mistrust that I ascended the pulpit if I had dared to reduce a paragraph here and there into a dozen words. But practice brings confidence and mastery, and with two sermons on Sunday and sometimes two in between, confidence slips in unawares.

I soon settled down to my work, my visiting and my care of the little mission church, which was quite holding its own if not a little more, and I was very happy. In reality neither of the two mission churches was needed at all; they were quite near the parish church and any church member worth his salt could easily attend the services of that church. The reason for their existence was obvious: there were in the parish two classes of people — the professional and the successful business man, who lived in the bigger houses away from the mills and the congested areas, and who attended the parish church. The other class was that made up of mill workers and their families, herded in these less salubrious streets, who appeared in caps, wore coloured handkerchiefs round their necks, and whose womenfolk went about in clogs and shawls. It had long been recognised that these people would not care to come and show themselves thus dressed before their more affluent brothers and sisters, so these two mission churches were built. It was a very sensible arrangement, based upon a realistic acceptance of the situation. And we did have women coming in in their shawls but not in their clogs, on Sunday, unless it was one of our more elderly members.

The mention here of clogs reminds me of my first few nights in the town when I was awakened by the clattering of clogs down the street, followed by a series of knocks on a window and the exchange of one or two muffled words — it was my first introduction to the 'knocker-up'. Very soon the street resounded to a hubbub of noise as clogs clattered and greetings of recognition were exchanged.

I am glad to say that I was trained to visiting, and to a regular number of visits, below which one would not dare appear at the Monday morning conference without a very good reason. The primacy of this work, established early in my ministry, has remained with me all my life as a duty and a discipline in which I have never allowed myself to relax. It is all very well to say, as many have said: 'Here is the church, the parishioners know where it is, and they know where the Vicar lives — if they need his help or his services, why can't they go to him as they go to the doctor, the dentist or the lawyer?' Yes, but to none of these had the parable of the lost sheep been spoken.

The young curate's visits were received almost everywhere with courtesy; I had a feeling that they accepted it as something they had a right to, and indeed, a right to all the help and the services the church was traditionally supposed to supply. To whom in those days could they talk so intimately about their children and their personal and domestic problems as to this young visitor who could then bring them to the notice of a church that had great experience and considerable resources to deal with acute and pressing problems? It must be remembered that many of the social services and agencies that all Local Authorities pride themselves on providing today, did not then exist.

In addition to taking charge of my mission church and district, the responsibility of visiting the workhouse also devolved upon me. I had had much experience in this sort of work at Pontypridd. Big as that was, this was a much bigger institution still, housing, apart from the sick, the aged and the poor, a large population of permanent inmates suffering from various kinds and degrees of disability; the spastic, the crippled, the weak-minded, the deformed. One's main work was in the sick wards. In addition to my regular visits I also went in response to notes that might be delivered to me any time of the day, stating that so and so was *in extremis*. One's mission here was to comfort the dying, by reading, by kind and soothing words, by prayer, and by touch of the hand — in all the ways known to pity and religion and love, to ease the departure of a brother or sister to whom life had been hard, sometimes so hard as to cause much misery and suffering.

This work will test to the utmost one's vocation, and one must pity the priest who in the least degree recoils from it. It is not the kind of work one would seek. Fortunately, it does not come often – one is not standing by sick beds, or death beds, every day. The greater part of a priest's work is pleasant and gives much pleasure: the work amongst the young, where there is fun and singing and laughter, and the many hours spent in friends' homes. Besides, there are the many social occasions, the days off, the walks into the country, and the pursuit of a few hobbies and studies that a young priest is already seriously giving his mind and his time to. I once gave a talk on the non-pastoral pursuits of the clergy.

One never knew what sort of reception he would have from the patient. I can recall one occasion when the man to whom I had been called seemed not to need me at all, but then doctors know best. My way of approach varied, but it often went like this: 'I hear you are not very well today, is there anything I can do for you? Would you like me to read to you or say a prayer? It would help both of us'. He replied, with a look, and a scowl to match, 'No. None of that for me'. I could not withhold some kind of admiration for him – so had he lived, and so he meant to die. I just made some casual remark such as that I hoped he would feel better in the morning, and moved away.

One of the saddest cases that I remember was that of a man who had once been the organist of one of the London churches. Then he lost his only child – a little girl – and from that moment he became a rebel against God, against the church, against life, and, if he only knew it, against himself. He took to drink, lost his post as organist, brought his wife to an early grave by his defiance and disorderly life, lost all self-respect and took to the roads. Broken in health, tired and worn out, he drifted in to Stockport Workhouse. He was very calm and very quiet now, the fiery rebellion had burnt itself out, the hot and bitter day was over and peace had come as the vesper bells called him to Evensong. He appreciated our chats together. He knew he was dying – his life was over, and he would tell his story quietly and honestly, without shame, without pride, as if he were relating the story of another person. He himself had died with his little girl; the mad, defiant, drunken creature that lived on was another person who had no more in common with the first that has a butterfly with the previous stage in its life's evolution. When we parted for the last time he knew that we should be together once again, just him and me — and so it was, when I committed his body to the ground and commended his tortured soul to the 'everlasting mercy' of Him who gave it.

And this brings me to speak of funerals. The reader must bear in mind the fact that I came from a land where the burial — the disposal — of the dead was from time immemorial a matter that concerned the whole community, and that community was prepared to give up the whole day to observe the customs demanded of the occasion. And in order that they might have early and ample notice of it, the family hired the 'official', or at least 'recognised' crier, or herald, to go round all the farms and cottages to give notice of the time and the place. Imagine therefore how strange and cold and mechanical I found these workhouse burials — human beings were disposed of with as little concern and sentiment as the disposal of a farm implement at a dispersal sale. In the funerals from my own mission district, there were plenty to accompany the dead, for there existed a very strong community feeling in all the streets. These again would be joined round the grave by at least an equal number of spectators, drawn from the normal crowd, mostly of working-class women, who used the cemetery as a park. So, between everything there was generally a considerable number round the grave. The women who joined us from the cemetery crowd must have come in response to the powerful appeal of this last scene in the final act of the drama of life, the same appeal that drew the whole primitive community to the burial mound to see one of their number being pushed in to the dark chamber, deep in its bowels. Far less laborious and far less dramatic is the act today — the mere dropping of the human body into the pit — but it still draws. These workhouse funerals were bare, cold and mechanical, just the priest, the deceased inmate, and the four bearers, all from the institution. Sometimes, two were buried together, and during the 'flu that followed the First World War, I remember burying four at the same time. Of course one had to get used to all this, bare, remote and impersonal as it was. Pathetic indeed was it when, occasionally, a stranger, in cap and cravat, hobbled up to the grave, stood mutely there, threw something into the grave, a token of remembrance of, perhaps, youthful and happier years — and moved away.

As it was war-time, I joined the Stockport company of the 9th Cheshire Volunteer Regiment and put in a lot of training in the evenings at the armoury there. On Saturdays we often went up to Ashby-de-la-Zouch for open-air rifle shooting, at which, having been used to the gun at home on the farm, I won many prizes, in the shape of pipes and tobacco pouches. In time I was given a stripe and was made a lance-corporal. I suppose they thought I deserved it. I offered myself as a chaplain but no call came — the war was then dragging towards its close.

At one time I became possessed of a silly idea, and that was that I could, since Manchester was so near, take another degree at the university there. I therefore sought an interview with Professor Tout who had once been on the staff of my old college. It became, however, immediately obvious that serving in such a large and busy parish as I was, I could not possibly put in the necessary attendance at the lectures. I never mentioned the matter to my Vicar at all; had I done so in the first place, it would have been disposed of quickly and finally. I suppose it could be done by a young man in one of the country parishes not far from the city, but just yet I did not want to return to the country. I am not sorry the idea came within the orbit of my early ambitions. Youth, if healthy and vigorous and enterprising, must entertain a few ambitions and dreams — dreams of mighty achievements, even of miracles!

SIX

Return to South Wales, and our first home

THE WAR WAS NOW OVER and I was a married man. It behoved me therefore to look out for another curacy, and a curacy with a house. I felt that now, having had three years at Pontypridd and three years at Stockport, I could look out for a curacy in charge, which was one degree above that of a mere assistant curate, and regarded as necessary to qualify for an incumbency. In reality, I had been in full charge of my district and mission church ever since I came to Stockport, but it still fell somewhat short of the charge of a consecrated church serving a clearly defined district, though it had hardly any connexion with the mother church, and little or no supervision from the Vicar.

The church, up at the top, and officially, did not concern itself at all with lesser breeds than incumbents — it appointed these and provided houses for them, and there it stopped. It is true that parishes, in view of the increasing number of married curates, had had to move on their own and provide houses for them. I was for some time in correspondence with a Liverpool incumbent, who felt sure he could get me a house by Christmas, but that did not seem to satisfy me at the time. Then I saw a curacy advertised in the *Western Mail*, which, in addition to a good stipend offered a house 'standing in its own grounds'. Though correctly described, it never came up to the first vision one formed of it on reading the advertisement. It was a small house, and an old one, but it was our first home and we were very happy in it. As I look back on the long road my wife and I have travelled together, and dwell over our stay here, the sun is always shining over that little house — and its grounds. On the strength of the house (including the grounds), everything else being quite satisfactory, I accepted it, and so in the year 1920 I returned to Wales — to the parish of Pontardulais, near Swansea, in the diocese of St David's. Very soon the diocese was divided and I found myself in the new part that was given the name of Swansea and Brecon. Pontardulais was then a large, straggling, industrial village of which there were many round Swansea and Llanelly. Its principal industries were coal, tin and iron works. And though there was an increasing number of English-speaking people in it, it was thoroughly Welsh in spirit and outlook, with Welsh as the language of the hearth, the places of worship, the mine and the floors of the tin and steel works.

I was sorry to leave Stockport. I was well settled in by now, knew my district thoroughly, and was happy with my people in the little mission church, which was more than holding its own. Besides, I had made many friends in the parish, so that it was a bit of a wrench to tear myself away and start all over again in a new place. I ought to make it quite clear that I felt no patriotic urge to return to my own country; there was no sense of guilt, and no uneasiness whatsoever in my mind, at having turned my back on my country. No consideration whatsoever pressed on my conscience, that as a son of Wales and of the Church in Wales, I ought to return to offer it my service once again — nothing of the kind. I had of my own free will crossed the border, like hundreds before me, for the English pulpit had exercised a tremendous attraction on the minds — some say on the conscience — of a lot of Welsh people. Of course, I loved Wales, loved to return to Wales, loved to hear Welsh singing and loved its wild romantic scenery. I revelled in this nostalgic feeling, in which a Cymric expatriate loves to bathe his soul. To return to Wales would be to lose all that, for one would be in possession of everything, and enjoying everything that gives rise to that nostalgic feeling, and the reality of what is longed for is a poor substitute for that nostalgia born of loss and deprivation, and nourished by it.

North country people were like my own in many things, they loved music, loved bands, loved singing, though as congregations they did not enter into hymn singing with all the abandon we did. They also loved sermons. 'Sermons' were a great occasion in Lancashire, they reminded me of our harvest festival sermons and the preaching sessions of Nonconformity.

I arrived in Pontardulais in the autumn of 1920 and as the miners' strike was on, there were a lot of people on the street. Along with my ordinary case I carried on my shoulder my golf bag, and it became the centre of much curiosity, guesses and remarks. Later on, I introduced the game to the town, and became the first chairman of the committee. After tea at the Vicarage, the Vicar took me for a short walk to show me the district which was to be my charge. When we came to a vantage ground, he pointed to a village about two miles away and said: 'I want you to take care of the church and people there'. I could not help thinking that compared with the massed streets of that district my Rector showed me in Stockport between those chimney stacks, this would be child's work, and yet experience bade me not to forget the shock I had over that district. Though it looked as if I could cover it all in a day, another, and altogether a new element entered into the situation, and that was the distance. Two miles three times a day, and the same distance back again, meant twelve miles, a pretty considerable Sabbath walking, and though I did not possess a bicycle, I was young and long-legged, and soon discovered that I could manage it very nicely and get much enjoyment out of it at the same time.

During the first month or six weeks in Pontardulais, I was in rooms, spending quite a lot of time getting the house ready and putting our few sticks in, with the very willing help of the men folk where I stayed. At last it was ready and my wife arrived, accompanied by her mother. We walked up all the way through the long main street of Pontardulais and when we got near the top, my mother-in-law said: 'what a lot of chapels'. They were beginning to get to know Wales. After we had turned in to the Goppa road, and were nearing our cottage, another chapel loomed into view, and they both exclaimed: 'Not another chapel'. Yes, it was the famous Goppa chapel, the Methodist Cathedral of the region. Another thing my wife soon tumbled to was the propriety of having the blinds lowered when a funeral passed; and many passed us, for the Goppa chapel had a large membership, and its own burial ground. I remember my wife and her mother watching through a chink in the blinds when the first funeral passed, and asking: 'Where do all these people come from?' They were learning. I did not say much to my wife about Wales and our way of life for the first month or so, for she was herself an observant girl, and I knew that the questions and the comments would come. The differences she found in coming to Wales were greater than those I encountered in going to England, besides, there was the difference of language. Her first impression of the people – and in her case of the women – was that they were less forthcoming, and kept more in reserve than North country people generally, but then she met others who poured out everything before her, so that she knew everything about them, from their grandmothers down, in addition to the aunt in America and the sister who had married that good-for-nothing fellow, etc. It was almost embarrassing. The fact is, and that I think explains best of all her experience of us, that in every place we ever lived in, early acquaintances ripened into friendships that she cherished to the end of her days.

For the first time in her life she heard Welsh all round her every day, but whether she knew at this time that it was an ancient language which possessed a rich literature of its own, or whether she thought it was one of the regional speeches of England, like that of Devonshire, Yorkshire, Dorset or Scotland, but because of centuries of isolation and separation it had retained archaic forms, and an old-fashioned vocabulary that made it today so very much unlike twentieth-century English, I don't know. But I don't think it could be otherwise, for her brother asked me one day if I could speak this 'lingo' that had survived in Wales, and I said I could. So for his benefit I recited a few sentences in Welsh; he didn't like to laugh out in my face, but a broad smile lit up his face as he asked me in utter astonishment: 'Where ever did you learn it?'

One Sunday evening soon after we arrived, my wife went down to the English church; it was a special occasion and the Bishop of St David's – Bishop Owen – was preaching. When she came home, I asked her how she had liked it and what she thought of Bishop Owen. Her reply was: 'It is no use my going to hear a Welsh sermon. I didn't understand one word he said' and the Bishop had been preaching in English all the time! Those who remember his very heavy Welsh accent, and the other defect which we in Welsh call *tafod tew* (thick tongue), will sympathise with her. Anyhow, whatever she thought of it, I am sure of this, that had we lived a few years longer in Pontardulais she would have quickly picked it up and the children as well, for she loved to watch the little children playing on the road in front of the house and she would come in and ask, what is *'fi gynta'*, what is *'paid'*: and many other words and phrases. Unfortunately we moved away to more anglicised parts.

She had other things to learn. One of them was the way in which we spelt and pronounced our place-names. She was stranded for hours in Swansea one day, waiting for a bus to a place we pronounced Pontardawey, but none came, though there were plenty going to a place called Pontardaw (spelt Pontardawe). However, before the last bus left, she discovered that Pontardawe was not Pontardaw but Pontardawe(y).

Brought up in a residential area outside Manchester, and on top of that the seclusion of a girls' school, she had not seen humanity in the raw, but seeing the miners coming up from the pits and seeing the men coming out of the tinplate and steel works, and exposing as they did so their heated, sweating bodies to the cool refreshing breezes, she discovered that most men had hair on their chests, in many cases matted masses of hair. Her own people were the light-haired folk of the North, and were deficient in this respect, and I, belonging to the red-haired folk, was more deficient still. She never told me anything at the time — it was my daughters who told me years afterwards. Perhaps she was sorry for me in that I lacked what must surely be the supreme and unrivalled token and proof of masculinity and virility!

Pontardulais again had the bilingual problem, but not in quite so pressing a form as in Pontypridd, for here the English immigration had not come in with such a tidal force as to swamp the native Welsh. Up till now, the Welsh had been able to absorb the majority of those who came into its own linguistic, social and religious framework. And what is more important, in that it obviated all resentment and sense of injustice on the part of the native Welsh in these growing industrial areas round Swansea and Llanelly, is, that they retained their hold on the parish churches. It was the in-coming English who had to worship in the church room or had to have a church built specially for them, which in any case would only have the standing of a daughter or mission church.

It was very different in the Rhondda: not only were the parishes so large and the churches so far apart that when this tidal wave of immigration 'bored' its way into the Rhondda, new parishes had to be formed, which in all cases, as far as I know, were to make provision for services in the English language, with the result that the parish churches from the first were the possession of the English-speaking people. These naturally held the primacy of authority and import- ance. In some cases they did, as a concession to the few Welsh-speaking members, build a mission church for them; but these realised from the first that they had only a secondary standing — the only matter in which they could make their voice heard was in the appointment of the Vicar. Their very existence determined that he should be Welsh- speaking, and so it can be said that the ministry of the church in Wales in Glamorgan and in South Wales generally, remained as Welsh as in the parishes of Cardiganshire and Carmarthenshire, and so, too, did remain the churchmanship and the general character of the preaching and teaching.

But to move back from the Rhondda: As time went on, these English or daughter churches grew rapidly in numbers, and before long became the church of the majority, having among its members a large number of the sons and daughters of those who were still loyal to the parish church, and who, though they may have had a smattering of Welsh, or indeed enough Welsh to follow a Welsh sermon, preferred to worship with the majority in the English church, which, invariably, was made up of younger people who were also more active socially and more enterprising in the number and variety of the activities they supported. Not only was it taking the lead in the activities of the parish, it was also by now the backbone of the financial strength of the parish, and yet despite all this, theirs had only the standing of a mission church, while that big beautiful parish church was in the hands of a declining Welsh congregation, whose wardens were the senior wardens. Things could remain like this for a very considerable time.

It is only those who have worked in bilingual parishes that realise how many problems it can give rise to. Nonconformity, not having the parochial system, accepted responsibility for the religious and spiritual care or oversight of only its own members. Welsh nonconformist churches catered only for Welsh-speaking people, but as changes came about, and the flow of immigrants increased, their conscience would not allow them to stand still and see them drift to the Anglican church or sink into paganism, so the *'Inglis côs'* began to be talked about and acted upon. These churches of the 'English Cause' took full responsibility for the English-speaking nonconformist population, leaving the Welsh or mother chapel to go its own way. Nonconformity therefore never knew the tension the parochial clergy experienced in trying to cater for the Welsh and the English and in trying to deal justly with both.

Many of these Welsh chapels, founded early in the industrial age, grew into very strong and influential churches, able to attract to their pulpits the most eloquent preachers of the time. Some were popularly known as the 'cathedrals' of their regions. Even when the district around them had become entirely English-speaking quite a few of these survived merely by *vis inertiae*, drawing their select congregation from a wide area. But the majority of the Welsh nonconformist chapels, though they soldiered bravely on, had to accept in the end the realities of the situation; and as the children were the first casualties of the change, the first concessions were made to the Sunday schools. Then, gradually, more and more English was introduced into the evening services, as they were frequented by a much higher proportion of the young. The morning service was now the only service conducted in Welsh, and this could remain the ordinary state of things until these old-timers faded at last away.

By holding out so determinedly against the surging tide of English, nonconformist places of worship acted as bulwarks of the language and its culture, and undoubtedly delayed its disappearance for a full generation. One admires their stand, but it cost them rather dearly in many places, for the fewer, and the tardier, the concessions they made, the stronger became the reasons of those who were losing their grasp of the language for joining the *'Inglis côs'* or the Anglican church. Nevertheless it is a fine and heroic chapter in the history of nonconformity.

Before I finish with the many and difficult problems that bilingualism gives rise to, and the very sensitive human strings it can touch, and often produce discord and wrangling, I must pay tribute to the patience, the wisdom and the infinite tact of the parish priests of Wales, and to the care with which they tried to deal justly with the situation. They managed to keep together the native and the newcomer, the Welsh-speaking and the English-speaking without outbreaks of rebellion — for feelings could run high — and without the formation of split churches, which so disgraced the history of nonconformity (not on the language question) in many places.

I must now say something of my Vicar, Canon W. Morgan, like myself, a Carmarthenshire man, and typical in many ways of the clergy who manned such bilingual parishes in industrial South Wales. He was born (1863) soon after the commencement of a great building era in the Church in Wales, in which churches, mission churches, church halls, church schools and vicarages were built at a rate never known before and one that was continued well-nigh up to the First World War. It had to be a church-building age, for immigrants were arriving in their thousands in South Wales; it incidentally shows that the church was quite alive to its responsibility to the people who were arriving in their parishes, not only to provide places of worship for them, but also schools for their children. This is a unique and heroic chapter in the history of the Church in Wales.

In any case it had to be a church-building era. Let us take as an example, Ystradyfodwg, that huge parish which comprised the greater part of the Rhondda. It experienced almost a Klondyke rush of immigrants, having been a barren hill-country with only a few farms in its secluded vales when Canon William Lewis came there in 1869. When he died in 1922 the parish had been divided and subdivided into thirteen parishes with twenty-four churches, all equipped with vicarages, church rooms and all the requisite means of running such parishes. (I am indebted to the Rev. T. J. Prichard, Vicar of Penygraig, for this information). The old Canon kept a day-journal which his foolish son destroyed, and so there perished for ever the thrilling story of one of the most exciting and rapid expansions in the history of the Christian church.

Canon Morgan had built an English church in Pontardulais, St Michael's, two mission churches, one at Pontlliw and the other at Grovesend, and also that very beautiful church at Gorseinon, which, since, has become a parish church, serving a new community which was attracted to the place when the Grovesend Steel Works was erected. The churches at Pontlliw and Grovesend were, it is true, timber and corrugated iron buildings, but they housed quite substantial congregations and flourishing Sunday schools. In addition, he and all like him had to get an extra staff, which meant, even though they got increasingly better grants (after all they were only grants), that the greater part of the money had to be raised in the parish. Yes, these clergy worked hard — an unorganised and unrelated body of forward-looking pioneers. A man was then judged by the number of churches he had built or renovated, and the money he had collected. Promotion came to those who could show concrete (i.e, in brick and mortar) proof of energy and achievement. I am sorry to say that I have lived long enough to see the emergence of a generation of clergy, utterly ignorant apparently of the primary need of the churches in that age of expanding industry and the arrival of new waves of immigrants — long enough to hear them contemptuously refer to these as 'brick and mortar clergy', being very careful to convey the impression that since they were men who dabbled in brick and mortar, they were therefore *ipso facto* unconcerned with the spiritual and with the deeper claims of religion. It is not true. I was privileged to know some of these men; it just happened that they were born to meet this rush of immigrants into South Wales, and how grateful ought we to be that they did so much dabbling in brick and mortar, for they could build at that time a school, a vicarage, a church or church hall, for a tenth of the money it would cost today. I am glad to pay this long-overdue tribute to them: the hard-working generation of Welsh clergy who provided practically all the parishes of Wales with churches, schools, vicarages, halls and all they needed for the efficient running of the parishes as understood in those days. They built churches and filled them. And I may say, too, that there was very definite church teaching in that age and a real and conscious effort made to build up the congregations in the doctrines of the church. I have seen too much of, and I owe too much to, the work of this generation of Welsh priests not to feel constrained to pay this tribute of gratitude to them. It may be that this unappreciative attitude towards the achievements of this church-building age is a natural and understandable reaction, in that, since there has taken place a woeful falling off in church attendance, the maintenance of the churches they built has become a burden too heavy to be borne by the dwindling congregations.

A lot of the old clergy were formidable creatures, and autocratic in their ways. They planned and worked alone. They seldom had at their side any man to encourage or second them in their daring projects. Churches were built before the money to pay for them was got together, and they ran great risks in borrowing money. They did not lack courage. And though the parishioners might admire their Vicar for his building activities, the attitude of many was: 'he started it, let him get on with it'. With years of this experience they had become accustomed to consult only themselves. When disestablishment became a reality, the church drew up a constitution in which provision was made for the formation in every parish of a church council. These lone handers ground their teeth and snarled at the very idea of them. To be reduced, in their own parishes, to be merely the chairman of a lot of people who, in the day of decision and anxiety, stood on one side was something that did not come easy to them. But they were human after all, and despite the impression the above description might make on some minds, they bowed to the new order, and became almost to a man reconciled to it. I have known them in the full autocracy of their power to sack choirmasters and organists on the spot, turn out choirs at only a minute's notice and cancel a church trip an hour before it was due to start. Parish priests had power in those days and they exercised it.

And yet the truth is, strange as it may seem, that despite their autocratic ways, these old clergy were very much liked by their people. Is it possible that their liking and admiration for them sprang from the fact that they *were* autocratic? For people like their Vicar to be Vicar: to be the head of the church in the parish; to act as such; to take the lead; and be master in his own house. If he doesn't, they may have had experience of what can happen — an ambitious family will push itself forward and begin to lord it over the Vicar and the congregation. And if there is anything a congregation hates, it is this, for it can create cliques and divisions and destroy its peace and harmony. In the end their contempt for the weak priest who has allowed it to happen will equal their deep distress as they contemplate the divided and warring household, that was once so united and happy. No, they like the Vicar to *be* Vicar.

I might as well here finish with my Vicar before I turn to speak of my visiting. I said of my Vicar at Pontypridd that he was a crack shot, so was my present Vicar, Canon Morgan. He liked to spend a day in the fields and the woods with his gun and his dog, and I was invited to accompany him. I was useful to carry the cartridges, the refreshments, the game and the rabbits as they fell to his gun, and more than once I was able to draw his attention to a movement in the bushes. It was nothing 'infra dig' or distasteful, I was asked to do; the invitation to accompany him to the fields was looked upon as an honour to me and as such I gladly accepted it, though I might have now and again (quite willingly) to play the part of a beater. I enjoyed these days in the field with him and I recall them with much pleasure — those sunny, warm, autumnal days, calm and hazy. We would select a suitable hedge for our sandwiches, where a firm and safe seat could be secured. Here, strangely enough, the talk would be not of sport, game or shooting, but of events in the clerical life of my Vicar. I was made the recipient of many secrets and confidences; I learnt how so and so got that living for which he was utterly unsuitable, and why so and so, an excellent man, was refused it. I had hints of what he really thought of the bishops, but what took up the greater part of the conversation was preaching, and sermons, for it must be remembered it was still the age of the great preacher. He himself was master of the *Hwyl,* that peculiar aid to preaching which is unique to the Welsh pulpit. I heard many scraps of the remembered, and much-thought of, sermons he had preached in his lifetime. I concluded that he took his hat off to no man in the Welsh pulpit at that time, when, as he said 'he took his coat off'.

The reader already knows that I am going to mention visiting again, but why? Well, because visiting in a north country town, and in England at that, is very different from visiting out in Welsh Wales. And I had to learn the hang of it again. In Stockport, the people were quite satisfied, possibly very pleased, with a short visit, the exchange of the usual courteous remarks, and the answering of a few questions, usually regarding the children and Sunday school, or choir attendance. Occasionally one might be detained, if more serious matters had been touched upon, otherwise I could get along and do quite a number of visits in one afternoon, but back here in Wales, a visit was a very different thing. In England I was all the time steering the conversation into the channels that I intended it should follow and I asked the questions and decided the length of the visit. In Wales I was by no means the master of my own visits, nor did I steer the conversation or ask the questions. Once I sat down I was taken possession of by the family, generally the mother. She hoped I would be very happy amongst them and stay long, not like my predecessor to run away after just four years, when they were beginning to get to know him. Was I pleased with the house? Was I married? In that case I must bring my wife round for them to see her. And, as if it was an afterthought, I must be dying for a cup of tea after walking those two long miles (actually, by making cuts, and following a straight line, I had been able to reduce them to one). While all this was going on I was held a prisoner in my chair. I tried, of course, to assert myself and explain that I had to get on as I had so many more people to see. It availed me nothing, and I gave in, for I was no match against a Welsh mother who was determined to possess me. The conversation, still steered by the mother, ranged far and wide: I heard all about her poor grandmother's last illness, who, poor thing, had she been allowed to live a few hours more, could boast she had reached ninety. I learnt about her brother in Australia, about her two sisters, one of whom had undergone a major operation recently, but was alive. I had to listen to little Gwyneth recite that piece which she had recited at the concert the previous week. Gwyneth was a little shy before the new curate, but after the usual childish show of refusal, recited her piece. I, a kind person by nature, feeling that I ought to be especially kind to children, praised her performance in very generous terms. This was a mistake; Gwyneth now lost all her shyness and wanted to recite all the pieces she knew, but her mother decided that with one more recitation she must be satisfied, for the afternoon, the whole of it, must be hers now that she had got the new curate with her — still in his chair. I had to look at endless photographs of the family; at certificates showing proficiency, or excellence, at various stages of piano-forte playing. I was shown the B.A. certificate — in a golden frame — of 'our Mary Ellen', first class honours in Greek and Maths: 'she's got brains has our Mary Ellen, the only first class at Aberystwyth that year'. As all this was being directed at me, I tried to remember that I was there to make a pastoral visit, to talk about the church, about church and Sunday school attendance, along with other kindred matters. I longed for the Hillgate district where I could do a dozen visits in that time. I got the hang of it again, and became quite happy if I could manage two visits, in an afternoon! When I really wanted to get on, I am afraid I had recourse to subterfuge, and made my visit between half past eleven in the morning and half past twelve, when dinner was being prepared and when, surely, no one would want to detain me. I found Friday, too, a good day to make some of my visits, for it would clash with shopping.

Not only had I to learn to do my visiting the Welsh way once again, but I had to learn also to take the funerals the Welsh way, and whereas I could bury four workhouse inmates in ten minutes in Stockport, if I could take one Welsh funeral in four hours I had no reason to complain. For one thing, South Wales is a place notorious for its unpunctuality. One of my lady-wardens in a conversation once told me that there were some people who if they could not be everywhere in time got so worked-up, so crotchety and nasty that there was no living with them. To her this urge to be punctual was a kind of affliction like asthma or rheumatism, but it well expresses the South Walian's attitude towards time. A funeral could well be held up for the best part of an hour because aunt Bess hadn't arrived, and the family dared not make a move until she arrived or else she would let hell loose on them. In the meantime the priest, if he is a bit of an anthropologist, can while away the interval in studying the physical characteristics of the relatives on both sides, for here the tribes come together. The aged great-grandfather is there, hobbling on two sticks, by his side is a boy of seven of the fourth generation, and he can't help noticing sufficient evidence already that when he grows up, he will be the very spit of the old man. If the ghosts of those early forefathers who, three thousand years ago, deposited their dead in the burial mounds on the hills around us, were looking down upon us they would feel quite at home.

We may as well finish with our visiting, too, while we are at it. I was not, of course, given every time I visited Mrs Jones the story of her grandmother's last illness, the story of the brother in Australia, nor that of the sister who had undergone that serious operation. Photographs and certificates were not shown every time, and so, gradually, I was able to get, occasionally, the reins back into my own hands, and these occasions increased in number and length as time went on. Mrs Jones, inventive and loquacious as she was, could run out of topics sometimes, and quietly I could get control of the conversation for considerable periods and make my choice of the topics, but the one thing I could not escape was the cup of tea — and you may be sure it was a nice cup of tea, with Welsh cakes, or something similar, to go

with it. Why couldn't I take it easy and enjoy my cup of tea!
But then I wanted to get on and do, if not a dozen, at least
one other visit. However, in Wales one must do one's visits in
the Welsh style, that is, one must be prepared to give more
time to each family, to listen to many more family matters
that will be touched upon, mainly concerning the educational
progress and achievements of the children. Why do our
parishioners take it for granted that the clergy will be — and
ought to be — interested in all this? There are hundreds of
years of history behind this universal assumption and attitude
of mind. Along the generations their parish minister was with
them on all occasions of sorrow or joy — their funerals as
well as their christenings and weddings. Old attitudes of mind
die hard. Until now, the Vicar is still a welcome visitor in the
homes of his people. But if the authorities tinker overmuch
with age-long communal boundaries, forget the value of
personal contact and acquaintance, and if the parochial
system is scrapped in favour of large Rectorial divisions,
worked from a centre away in the market or county town,
the church and the ministry may become as impersonal as the
Post Office of the Income Tax Office, and the man to whom
the spiritual charge of the parish has been committed may be
as much a stranger to his people as the chief Education
Officer — unless by some chance the oversight of the parish
has been committed to a part-time postman and part-time
priest. It may not matter so much after all, for I hear on all
sides that no visiting is done today. How this came about I
don't know, unless it can be attributed to the mushroom
growth of theological colleges in the nineteenth century,
presided over by men who knew little or nothing of the
pastoral work of the ministry. At last the church, after the
manner of the good husbandman, had taken the hoe into its
hand and has started thinning out in this section of the field.

Quite a few of the people the parson visits are miserable
people, people who live their lives with complaints — and
indeed would seem to be happy to have complaints. There
must be few clergy who have not heard this sort of thing in
their time: 'What a poor congregation last Sunday, Vicar, I
don't know what the church is coming to, so very different
from what things were in old Mr Jones's time. You had then

to be in church half an hour before the time or else you would not get a seat. But then he was such a wonderful man. Such a fine preacher, such voice and such a commanding presence'. There are many ways of countering such attacks: one is to agree with them and say that you hear from neighbouring clergy and ministers that the same thing is happening in their churches; another is to look into things to see if what is said is really true. I found myself once up against this very thing in one of my mission churches, which, as it happened, was at the time in quite a flourishing condition, but nothing like what it was in the old days, which they all loved to recall: the time when you had to go to neighbours' houses to borrow chairs for the packed congregation. Fortunately the church registers were available, and I looked up the record for those years so fondly remembered, and I was surprised to find that, if anything, our number of communicants, and the amounts of the collections, were higher now than in the years they boasted of. What happens in such cases is that special occasions such as harvest festivals are the ones that stand out in their memories, and having been so fondly dwelt upon in recollection, the mind has come to accept them as the normal occasions, whereas the ordinary Sunday attendances, lacking this impressive crush, failed to register on their minds, and are clean forgotten.

Before he goes very far somebody will complain to him of the terrible draught in the church, especially where the complainant is sitting: 'It is terrible, Vicar, and I am not coming to church again until you do something about it'. The Vicar may suggest that she (of course there are male complainants as well) moves forward and sits in the pew with Mrs Evans: 'There's plenty of room there, and Mrs Evans has never complained of the draught'. That did it! 'Me, sitting next to that woman. No, thank you, Vicar. I haven't forgotten yet how she snubbed me at the tea-party. No, I am not going to give up my seat to please anybody. I have sat there all my life, and my parents and grand-parents before me'. The Vicar tactfully agrees with her and says that neither would he give up a seat that can claim so long and honourable a tenancy.

He most certainly will have to meet complaints about the

choir — and in more than one house: 'Can't you do
something about the choir, Vicar? If I were you I would sack
the lot, the organist as well, and begin to build up afresh
from the bottom. And, by the way, Vicar, who chooses the
hymns? In addition to a poor choir, must we also have
miserable hymns? Let's have a few bright hymns with a bit of
go about them'.

In the next house is the man with the watch. Whenever he
is travelling by bus or by train he's always got his watch out,
and has been heard to say amongst other things: 'This train is
on time for once'. With the Vicar the preliminaries are few,
and he pitches at once into battle: 'Vicar, you preached for a
solid thirty-five minutes on Sunday evening. I am not saying
that it wasn't a very good sermon, but thirty-five minutes,
Vicar! I reckon that a man ought to be able to say all that
needs to be said on any text in fifteen minutes'. The Vicar
humbly agrees with him that he, too, thought it was a good
sermon, but that he was carried away in the fervency of his
spirit and forgot all about the time. What made him oblivious
of the time and of everything else was the look of expectancy
on the faces of the people as they rivetted their upturned
faces on him, urging him to go on and on and on. In a nice
way the man with the watch will be made to feel that he was
the only one that was out of tune, striking a jarring note in
the harmonious blending of all hearts and minds in the
offering up of that evening worship.

Then there used to be the man who was a stickler for
verbal loyalty and obedience to the Prayer Book and its
rubrics. A man who believed in the verbal inspiration of the
1662 Prayer Book. A Prayer Book fundamentalist. An angle
of it can be seen when I say that I was once asked by one of
my people: 'Vicar, isn't the Prayer Book good enough for us
these days? Why bring in all those prayers about industry, the
League of Nations, unrest in South America and prayer for . .
. . .? The Prayer Book knows nothing about these things. We
shall soon be like nonconformists and pray for everything
and everybody. We might as well join them and throw our
Prayer Book overboard'. This loyal old type, narrow certainly, but with many excellent qualities, has now been
eliminated by the church itself in its many *series,* for one

cannot be loyal to changes — it doesn't make sense.

The person most difficult to deal with is the person who is more clerical than the clergy, more priestly than the parish priest. Is he affecting the pose of holier than thou? At any rate he lets it be known that he keeps more holy days, fasts longer, keeps more of the 'hours', observes more saints' days, even the days of obscure saints from outlandish parts of the world, men — or women — hardly deserving of a footnote in the wide historic study and balanced reading of church history. He may in addition have made a study of, or, worse still, read one book, again on some obscure point in liturgy or theology, which his Vicar could have shown to be of such little significance that neither his tutors, nor the authors of the books they recommended, even so much as mention the point. Such people are widely met with in this world: Lawyers are familiar with this type, the person who comes to see them apparently only to air his knowledge of law to them; the doctor has met him too — the person who knows what is wrong with him and disagrees with his diagnosis; the passenger who knows better than the staff how to run the train service. Such folks can be very awkward — and they certainly are to be found in our churches.

In the course of a month's visiting, the Vicar will have come across all these complaints and many more, but in most cases, once they've got the complaint off their chest, the rest of the visit can be quite pleasant indeed. Most clergy are wise enough to know that, and to allow for it. At the end of his round of visiting he is glad he said so little, and that he had the grace and the strength to shut up, even when he knew he would be quite justified in saying what he felt like saying. If he took notice of everything, and decided he would not call on that particular family again, he would very soon be reminded: 'Vicar, you haven't been round to see us lately'. Well, when all is said and done, these are his people, these are the people he has been put in pastoral and spiritual charge of, these are the people he prays for — 'the all sorts and conditions', so he might as well get to know them in all their complaints, shortcomings, failings and human good nature. After all the years, he is still their Vicar, he still visits, the draught still blows over that seat, he still reaches the thirty-five minutes when he loses himself in his subject, the choir is still there, the complaints have ceased — or at least most of them, for what's the use! He could take very much more than at first they thought, and survive!

I hope I am not giving the impression that the Vicar is surrounded by a lot of sour, difficult and complaining folk. Of course he isn't. Looking back over fifty years of visiting, I must say I have very happy memories of a very pleasant part of my work, but I had to mention the character of the complaints the parish priest met with, when visiting was done, if my reminiscenses have any claim to be of value. The Vicar, unless he is an oddity, is generally a very popular person in the parish and indeed in a considerable area around. He enters more intimately into the lives of his people than do members of any other profession, and so much that happens in their own homes happens also at the Vicarage. That is the reason, I think, why parishes invariably prefer a married priest. I myself, and I daresay others too, have been amazed at the interest that is taken in the domestic events at the Vicarage, and the Vicar may be informed by a dozen mothers before the week is out: 'Yours is the first child to be born at the Vicarage', or, as happened in my case: 'Yours is the first boy to be born at the Vicarage'. And as the Vicar in his reading ranges over a far wider field than his parishioners, his fancy may be taken by a name from early Welsh history or even from legend, for his little daughter — *Angharad* perhaps. If the folks like it, and they probably will, in about a month he will be baptizing little Angharad baby girls, and may go on doing so for ten years. He and his wife will note this tribute with considerable satisfaction.

SEVEN

To Swansea Valley – and sole charge

IN THE LAST CHAPTER I said I had jumped forward over the years in order to say all I wanted to say about visiting, but I must now return to my curacy at Pontardulais: In a month or so after arriving in the parish, I had to make a visit to the Bishop of the diocese, Dr John Owen of St David's, to receive my licence. The interview took place at the registrar's office at Carmarthen. When I was ushered in he was sitting at his desk, writing. Without looking up he said: 'sit down' and went on writing; after a short time he finished writing, and looking up said: 'Ah, Mr Parry-Jones. Welcome to the diocese'.

'Thank you, my Lord', I said.

'I see you come from stockport. Who was your Vicar?'

'The Rev. Henry Sewell', I said.

'Ah, an old pupil o' mine'.

He remembered him after all these years. He was noted for his long and detailed memory, for his shrewd insight into character, belied by the fact that being heavy-lidded he gave one the impression he was half asleep. He was the most truly, typically, Welsh of all the Bishops Wales has ever had: a block of Welshness hewn from the solid rock of that Pre-Cambrian range that outcrops in the north, served in Wales all his life except for a short period after he graduated: knew the Welsh character as few have known it: nursed his Welsh accent, and as he used it you were reminded of the rugged landscape of the Welsh hills. To Welsh churchpeople of his day, he became, by reason of his epic leadership in the fight against Disestablishment, much more than a mere bishop, he became a champion, a commander, a hero. Wales had never known such a redoubtable cleric since Giraldus Cambrensis in the twelfth century.

When a considerable saga gathers round a person it is proof that he has arrived, better still if, as in the case of the Bishop, he has acquired a nickname. It is proof, too, of his general popularity. He had a far better opportunity of knowing his clergy than any of the other Welsh bishops as he had had a large number of them under him as Warden of Llandovery college, as Principal of St David's college, and, earlier, during a spell as professor of Welsh there.

Though my bishop was a Welshman, proud of his language and of his country, and I, a Carmarthenshire man, equally proud of my country and my mother's tongue, the whole interview was conducted entirely in the English language. I never spoke in my own native tongue to any Welsh bishop until I was over eighty years of age! I would not dare do so. But one day — in 1972 — I saw back in Newport the present Bishop of Llandaff (the Rt Rev. Stephen Thomas) and I plucked up enough courage to ask him in our common and native tongue how he was settling down in his new home. I was a little nervous, and very conscious of the strangeness of the step I was taking, not that I for one moment thought that he would resent it, but because of the novelty of what I was about to do. I needn't have had any anxiety at all, as I very well knew, for he answered my question — asked in the accents of *Sir Gâr*, (Carmarthenshire) — in his native speech of *Sir Fôn* (Anglesey).

Those few words are words to remember, for they are the first native words uttered to my Father in God in all my life. English people will marvel at this, and well they may, and wonder how came it about that an ancient tongue, the mother and medium of a rich and ancient literature and culture, should be so despised, looked down upon, and regarded as too common a medium of communication in learned and polite society. English clergy may well wonder what sort of church the Church of England would be if priests dared not speak to their bishops in the low-rated, second-class speech used by their flocks, but only in Latin or French. English people and the English church must take a share of the blame for this state of things, in that through their elected representatives in Parliament they decreed that in all official departments of Government, and especially in the important department of Education, our language should be officially ignored as something it was beneath their contempt to take notice of. And it was under the sway and active application of such ideas I was as a child educated — through a medium that was utterly alien to me, a tongue of which I knew not one word, as strange as would German be at that time to an English child. Would English parents submit to a system of education which prohibited as its medium the child's first and only language?!

In order to make it plainer still why I dared not speak to my bishop in our common tongue, let me illustrate it by what would be an exact parallel: Suppose a curate or a priest discovered that his bishop like himself hailed, say, from Yorkshire or Devonshire, and presuming on that fact began to talk to his Lordship in the dialect of that county. His bishop would most certainly resent it, even though both might be quite familiar with it. Dialect was all very well in a rural community where all knew one another very intimately and were all on the same social level. But away from that setting and between two who differed greatly in status, the use of dialect would imply that the speaker expected the other to respond in the same friendly, breezy manner as prevails amongst dialect speakers. The bishop would regard it as an affront and would soon show that such impertinence was not to be tolerated. And so exactly was it with the use of the Welsh language. My bishop knew as well as I did why I did not speak to him in Welsh, and respected me for it. This at that time applied not only to bishops, but to all Welsh people who considered themselves above those who were speaking to them.

If Doctor Owen were today Bishop of St David's and I a curate seeking a licence, he would almost certainly have greeted me in Welsh, for such is the change that has come over Wales in its attitude to the Welsh language. It has acquired a new status and a new dignity. As a result of neglect and suppression in all government departments, a large number of our people had come to accept the official

English view and estimate of Welsh as very much a second-class language, with only a limited use, as, for instance, in the service of religion, as a means of daily communication in a simple and somewhat primitive rural society, and in folk poetry and singing such as was indulged in at our national gathering — The Eisteddfod. But out of the sixth forms, out of our university colleges, there has come a continuous stream of dedicated teachers and scholars, men and women with a wide knowledge of the languages and cultures of other nations, who, in class, through the medium of books and periodicals, and in such lectures up and down the country as those sponsored by the extra-mural departments, have spread widely a new knowledge and a new appreciation of our language and of the culture it was and is the medium of. The change is so great as to be almost incredible. We have now a solid mass of instructed and enlightened people who have recovered their pride in their language. And whereas it was once thought to be only fit for peasant communication, the Welsh pulpit and exercises in peasant poetry, recent publications have shown that it is rich enought to treat of any subject from rugby to electronics. Scholars have given us in the last few years abundant terms in every discipline: terms formed from the abundance of root-words the language possesses and which show its unlimited possibilities of expansion.

How can we withhold our pride in our ancient tongue, a speech that has refused to die, though for many centuries it found itself up alongside a very powerful and unsympathetic neighbour, yes, a neighbour that has done its best at all times to eradicate and destroy it. Even when we were permitted to have the scriptures in our own language, that again was seen as an opportunity for readers to study the two versions, and by comparing them, the more easily to learn English. But God in his providence decreed that it should have exactly the opposite effect. What it did do was to set a literary standard that ruled unquestioned for over three hundred years — until Sir John Morris Jones produced his massive work on the language in the 'twenties of this century. Not only that, but, as knowledge of the scriptures became so widespread after the establishment of the Circulating Schools by the Rev.

Griffith Jones and the religious awakening that followed it —
to be followed in its turn by the establishment of Sunday
schools — its influence percolated through to the mass of the
people, providing them with a national medium, uniform in
speech, vocabulary, grammar and orthography which rose
above regional usage and indeed did much to prevent the
hardening of local dialects.

Here, I must leave the question of the language and return
to my curacy at Pontardulais. Two little girls were born to us
here, and whenever I recall those years, the sun is always
shining over that little home, 'standing in its own grounds'.
Domestic and family duties fell to my lot now as well as
pastoral duties, and in a very short time I got to know all
about babies; for example, how to hold them, which came in
very handy to me at the font. Many a clergyman has made a
mother's blood run hot and cold as she sees the casual,
clumsy way he holds her baby. I have since taken some pride
in my absolute competence in this important matter, and no
mother has ever had to hold her breath while her baby is in
my charge. And though I have never made a show of my
competence in this matter, I have not been unwilling for it to
be seen that I know all about it. The great secret is to give
always plenty of support to their heads. My wife and I were
extremely happy with our little ones though of course it gave
her very much more work. It meant, too, much more
expense, and we were still on a curate's pay of £3 a week. It
is a great temptation here to embark on the perennial and
vexed question of the parson's pay. We have with us, still,
those who believe that like the disciples we ought to serve the
church voluntarily and without pay; and there are those who
maintain that at three pounds a week, we were just doing
that. It will surprise nobody therefore that after three years
in Pontardulais I should begin to look for a curacy which
offered a higher stipend, and I found one in Swansea Valley,
in the parish of Llansainlet. It was a curacy-in-charge and
carried with it a stipend of £180 a year — an increase of £30,
which was a very substantial sum when the pound was worth
twenty shillings. The community that I was to take charge of
was the village of Glais at the top end of the parish of
Llansainlet. Here again we had a house 'standing in its own

grounds' but a much bigger and more modern house, with two bay windows. The little mission church had once been a barn but had been converted into quite a cosy, compact church, where gathered a very faithful congregation with a better choir and better singing than, I should say, in any daughter church in the whole of Wales, better even than in a large number of parish churches. It had a large Sunday school and a very faithful body of teachers.

In Glais, I was really a curate-in-charge: the village was right up at the top corner of the parish, and as it was not easy of access from the direction of the Vicarage, the Vicar never visited us except on such occasions as harvest festivals. Why should he be trotting up all the time: he had put what he considered an experienced man in charge and it was now his responsibility. However, every Monday morning the curate-in-charge was reminded that he was still a man under authority and was expected to attend the Monday morning conference at the Vicarage along with the other two curates.

Like Pontardulais, the village was unmistakeably Welsh in language and character, but with a growing number of English speakers, made up of English families whose wage-earner worked at the Mond Nickel Works, and young people who were beginning to show preference for the English language. Its overwhelming Welshness will be apparent when I say that its two nonconformist places of worship held their services entirely in Welsh — they escaped therefore the problem which faced us here again as it faced every other parish in South Wales, namely, the bilingual problem: how to accommodate, without causing a sense of injustice, the two groups within the one church and at the same time maintain a consciousness of a united congregation. The local solution, introduced long before my time, was one that worked very well — the Welsh had their service in the morning and the English in the evening and also an early celebration at eight o'clock. The Welsh might have preferred an evening service, but the certain prestige that belonged to the morning service more than made up for any sense of grievance they might have harboured in being pushed as it were to the less popular end of the day. It also for that reason denoted original ownership and primacy. Though the English congregation might now outnumber them, the possession of the morning service was a reminder to them that it was only by the good will and brotherly feeling of the native Welsh that they were accommodated at all. It was the usual morning congregation, made up mostly of elderly people; hardly any children at all attended. There was no choir, for those present thought of themselves as being choir as well as congregation. The surpliced choir turned up only in the evening, made up in part of Welsh-speaking members, and indeed a large number of the Welsh congregation turned out again in the evening. Despite the fact that it was made up of two congregations, it was a very happy and united church. As the English-speaking congregation had been allotted the evening service it involved as a consequence an evening communion. It was something new to me and though it branded us as the lowest of the low as far as churchmanship was then regarded — though I myself had a slight inclination towards a richer ritual — still I must say I enjoyed those communion services immensely; very likely a strong choir, good singing and a full church had much to do with it. A writer in *The Church Times* (May 1945) said that there were still a number of evening communions in Wales. May it not be due to the fact that we had, as in Glais, to accommodate two congregations, speaking different languages in one church building? As for the churches out in Welsh Wales, they had never heard of an evening communion: it was always at the morning hour of ten, taken over largely now by the family communion that has become so popular in England. I was conscious that the *spikes* amongst my fellow curates, whispered behind their hands to each other: 'Look who's coming, he has evening communion' as if it was something as horrible as having the leprosy. Then suddenly after the Second World War, the church of Rome, which they had been aping all along, cut the ground from under their feet, by going *low church* itself and introducing evening communion.

After three very happy years in Glais I thought it was time I should make some definite move to get a living. The authorities were apparently quite happy to let things go on as they were. I had now been twelve years in Orders and was a married man with two growing children. Though long curacies of this kind were nothing out of the ordinary in those days, yet contemporaries of mine had already settled down in their parishes. My first move was to mention the matter to my Vicar and as the Bishop was visiting the parish in a few weeks, he said he would speak to him about it. I met the bishop this day, and after tea we were left on our own for a few minutes when the matter was discussed. I noticed that the bishop was a very different person with me from what he was a few moments earlier with the Vicar. Gone was the free, light-hearted conversation; he had become reserved, more on his dignity, cautious, very much the bishop. There was nothing wrong with that, it was just something that I could not help noticing. After all I was only a curate and as this was our first meeting, I could not expect to be greeted and treated with the same freedom and in the same breezy manner as that which comes so natural to old colleagues, for the bishop had been for the greater part of his life a Breconshire parish priest. There was, his Lordship said, only one vacancy at the moment — and he mentioned it, that of Llan-Fawr. In justice to his memory I ought to say that he did not offer it to me. Though himself a bachelor who knew little of the problems and needs of family life, he must have realised it was no place to send a young man with a family to. Llan-Fawr was a parish in the hill-district on the north western fringe of Breconshire, remote, and sparsely populated. It had been described to me once by one who had served some months there as a *locum* after the First World War, as covering 20,000 acres, grazing 10,000 sheep, with a population of one person to every 40 acres. At this distance of time I should not like to press too insistently the accuracy of my figures, but they are guardedly given, as memory has retained them, but whether my friend was equally on his guard against exaggeration, I am not sure. Looking back over the years, I think now that my bishop was a merciful man in that he did not offer it to me, or ask me to go there. I escaped this time, but the possibility, nay, the probability, now dawned upon me that I should ultimately have to go, and take my family with me, to some such isolated country parish. It was not a happy prospect, for my wife until her marriage had lived with Manchester as the focal point of the family's shopping, entertainment and social life.

Visions and inspired thinking have seldom been vouchsafed to the Church of England; if it had, how very differently the matter of these hill-parishes could have been tackled. At this time it was the custom, in advertising for curates, for certain parishes to be described as 'desirable spheres'. If that is a true description of some parishes, others can equally truthfully be described as 'undesirable spheres'. Suppose the church had had the vision to pick out, say, half a dozen of the most isolated, least desirable parishes in the diocese and hold them up before the young and the courageous as a challenge worthy of their faith and their dedication — spheres involving some of the drawbacks, discomforts and the lack of modern amenities such as are met with only in the mission field — there would be no dearth of applicants. The challenge should be safeguarded by a provision that it should not exceed three or five years, unless the volunteer himself should wish to extend it. If that had been the case, I and others like me could have been thrilled with the offer of Llan-Fawr.

Unfortunately, at this time in the Church in Wales, it was widely accepted, if only in a casual and uncritical manner, that the parish reflected the character of the priest in charge — if he was in a small parish with a small population, he was a small man, if on the other hand one had a large and populous parish one was a big and important man. This sort of attitude to men and their charges had never been allowed, as far as I can make out, to infect and mar the life and mission of the nonconformist churches, for, there, great men had enhanced the name and honour of quite small and undistinguished little chapels, so that they outshone larger chapels in the big towns in popular estimation and appeal. They did not subscribe to the doctrine then prevalent in the Welsh Church.

In pre-disestablishment days things were very different. With the variety of patronage then existing, clergy were enabled to move from one diocese to another, and, as frequently, across Offa's Dyke. Besides, stipends were not so carefully graded according to the population of the parishes, the number of their churches and their general character, and many a parish, far in the country, had accumulated by various means a large and 'desirable' income, such as to

attract priests who had been better brought up than the
general run of us Welsh-speaking clergy. They were invariably
graduates of the older universities, and a few belonged to the
minor gentry class, and could, on account of their ignorance
of Welsh, be accommodated only in Radnorshire and South
Pembrokeshire. These fitted in very well into country
parishes, for they would already have country interests, such
as shooting and fishing, and would probably own a sturdy
mount if not a carriage and pair. The poor and undesirable
parishes in those days were the large industrial parishes,
struggling hard to provide for the spiritual needs of a growing
population and generally always in debt. Then came Disestablishment, involving widespread and radical changes.

I was brought up in an Established church, and though the
Disestablishment bill was passed in the year of my ordination, the delay of putting the act into execution on account
of the war meant that I served for six years in a church that
still functioned as an Established church. So I was there when
the big changes came about and was able to note the reaction
of the church, clerical and lay, to them. It must be
remembered that I am now talking about the years immediately after Disestablishment, when the church threw away so
much of the old harness in which it had worked along the
centuries. New harness was put on, and until we got used to
it, it hurt in places and, even as in the case of young horses
where the collar pressed hard, sores appeared. The system of
patronage was new and had not yet been tested. Elections
were introduced and a number of new boards, bodies and
committees were created. Naturally they attracted a large
number of ambitious people who like to work on committees. There was a great deal of bustle and much activity
of a kind — and much watching and wondering as the new
machinery jerked into action.

There existed a very widespread and genuine apprehension
at the time amongst us younger clergy who were looking
forward to a benefice as our next move and not to another
curacy. It arose largely from the nature and geographical
character of the diocese. It looks awkward and shapeless on
the map and can hardly ever acquire the sense or feeling of
itself as a homogeneous unit such as characterizes, for

example, the much larger diocese of St David's. I have never met anybody who is satisfied with it as a diocese. Apparently it was created to lighten some of the work of the Bishop of St David's, to give some relief to the overloaded diocesan machinery, and, possibly, not without the thought that since separation was forced upon us, it would be more agreeable to our national pride if we could boast that ours was a Province of six and not just four dioceses.

The diocese is made up of the town (now, city of Swansea) and the countryside around, with its long-established, industrialized villages, and one long valley, again largely industrialized, so narrow in places that in one part it comprises the width of only one parish. Soon after it enters Breconshire it spreads out to embrace the whole county, mostly a county of hills, upland farms and scattered villages. On top of this it takes in the whole of Radnorshire, a mid-Wales county partaking of the topographical character of that area. It never acquired, as I said, a feeling or consciousness of itself as a unit and I believe never can. There has been some talk of forming a mid-Wales diocese, and reviving the ancient claims of the see of Llanbadarn Fawr. Monmouth is the only diocese in Wales that can be said to be territorially satisfactory. What we need is the creation of two or three new dioceses and to relate boundaries more realistically to modern population movements and industrial expansion. The age of settling boundaries for hundreds of years is gone; there is no reason, in view of the establishment of new towns — and new industries — that there should not exist in the province a permanent body charged with giving easement and adjustment to parish and diocesan boundaries as the need arises.

Our apprehension and discontent as young men arose because of the vast contrast between the top and the bottom part of the diocese. Our prospect in the diocese pointed clearly to the fact that we should have to go to the hill-country. There was no hope of having a benefice in the southern, industrial area — those already there were sitting tight, and were determined that they were not going to be *buried alive* (that was the phrase we all used) in the hills of Brecon and Radnor. And that of course is what happened. One old clergyman stuck it out and kept his diocesan appointments until he was ninety and over. Naturally we were dissatisfied and discontented — and who can blame us: we were young, we had served ten or twelve years in the ministry as curates, and in the course of those years had acquired much experience, and were now looking forward to the time when we could put that experience at the disposal of our parishes, and put into practice certain ideas, experiments and methods, we felt sure would help to solve some of the problems of the church, and strengthen its hold upon the loyalty and devotion of its people, especially of the young. If we were sent into the isolated hill country where there was no population and no young people, our plans would have to be folded up and put aside, possibly for ever. Of course we were disappointed and discontented, if it were not so we would not be worthy of our youth. The authors of the jubilee brochure admit that the contrast between the 'wealthy, heavily industrialized area' round Swansea and the 'large rural area' has 'caused tension in the past'. Is it any wonder that some degree, or aspect, of this tension should be reflected in the minds of the junior clergy?

As things were at that time, the early 'twenties of this century, to face life in these sparsely populated counties was a grim prospect, for apart from Brecon, the hub of the diocese, with its many church meetings and gatherings and therefore the odd chance of meeting an interesting or entertaining cleric, there remained only Llandrindod Wells and a few market towns such as Builth, Knighton and Rhayader. These offered nothing to an intellectually inclined priest in the form of a good library or a good bookshop, much less did they have a group of people of like interests with himself, but they were quite good centres for household shopping.

I do not think that this problem confronted any other diocese in Wales. Even St David's, which is largely an agricultural area, has yet an evenly-spread uniformity about it. Cardiganshire, which might be considered outlandish, has Aberystwyth as its chief centre, a town with many attractions and activities to enliven the days, and focus the interests of its surrounding people; besides it is the locale of one of our university colleges, and of the National Library, where a priest of a studious nature can have plenty of help as well as the society of other minds in tune with himself.

Some may say that I am not painting a very nice or a very attractive picture of the church and the clergy of those days. It may be I am not, but so it was. I must describe things as they were and as they appeared to me. But I must guard against giving the impression that we, the senior men amongst the unbenificed, had our minds filled only with thoughts and prospects of promotion. Nothing of the kind. We worked too, and worked hard. Of course we dreaded — what eventually came upon us — being sent into the country. The prospect of having to spend the best years of our life in small thinly-populated parishes where we would not have the material — especially the young — to continue our work amongst, was indeed one that had little attraction for us. Nevertheless, we kept on working, so did all the lay people; how else does the reader think that a disestablished, robbed and crippled church moved smoothly and successfully, through that period of transition, gathering efficiency as it worked its way out of controls, restrictions, trappings, customs and structures that had built themselves up in the course of the centuries. It threw away the old harness in which it had worked for centuries and got a new set designed to give more ease and freedom and power.

Somebody one day will come along and, in a worthier manner than I am doing here, pay a just and adequate tribute to the men who manned the parishes in the first two decades after the Disestablishment and the laypeople who so loyally and bravely upheld their hands. Belts were tight at the vicarages: we knew nothing of the affluence and the handshakes that have come since. We expected little and were almost surprised that we got as much as we did. And though it was not the custom then for our wives to go out to work to implement the family budget, I never heard of anyone deserting the ministry or seeking posts in teaching or in television work, where the emoluments were very much higher.

I don't think the present generation can visualise quite what life was like in the 'twenties of this century — just after the devastation of the First World War — that is why I am going to say a little more about it: Very few clergy, if any, had cars — I cannot at the moment recall any — buses were beginning to appear, running to the larger towns from the surrounding villages, picking up passengers anywhere on the way — there were no set 'stops', but one was generally right in standing where a by-road emerged on to the main road, or where one saw a group of people standing. Our radio was in the cat-whisker stage, unless you were a rich man and could keep up with the latest experiments.

However, the world was soon to see one of those changes — one of those leaps forward — that left nothing the same again: I am referring of course to that great benefactor of humanity — Henry Ford — who at this time produced a motor car within the reach of the working man, and men like the clergy who were within the same wage bracket. At one stroke the isolation of the countryside vanished, and miles were seen to be reduced to yards as in the closing up of a geological concertina. Wales, still largely made up of rural parishes, was a country that benefited immensely. Later on, after the Second World War, there came another change, again not on account of any vision on the part of the church, but an innovation forced upon it by sheer necessity — the lack of ordained ministers to fill the parishes. Hence it had to experiment with amalgamating parishes, with the happy result that young men in country parishes were at last given something like adequate work to do, than which there is no better antidote to boredom, and the nursing of grievances.

Later on the church began to experiment with Rectorial parishes, where a number of clergy form a kind of parochial staff to work a group of parishes. As the coming of the car obviated the sense of isolation of the country priest, so did the Rectorial parish remove his sense of loneliness. Besides, rewards and emoluments have since been much more justly distributed, so that country charges are no longer looked askance at, nor the country priest looked down upon as a second-class priest. No longer is fun made of us when we attend church conferences (say in mid-summer) by asking us if the snow has already melted in the parish, or what sort of lambing season we had.

Town and country clergy — and their wives — often discussed the question whether it was cheaper to live in the town or in the country. Generally it was conceded that

taking everything into consideration most of the advantages
were with the townsman. But maids were cheaper in the
country, for mothers liked their girls to start as near home as
possible and to have some experience before they moved on
to the hotels at Llandrindod, or to the larger country houses.
Though the calls on the country parson's purse for charitable
appeals and organized occasions were fewer, yet his contrib-
utions had to be much more substantial, for in these matters
he was ranked with the gentry. The country clergyman's
fishing was deemed to be cancelled out by the townsman's
access to golfing. In this respect it is of interest to turn again
to Llan-Fawr, to which a young man went with his wife and
children. He told me that on every ton of coal brought up to
the Vicarage he had to pay one guinea for haulage. The
inevitable result was that he moved up to the North of
England and a devoted priest was lost to the church in Wales.
But it was in the matter of personal and special shopping, in
the matter of entertainment and in the field of cultural and
social activities, that the disadvantages became so obvious
that no comparisons could be made. Another matter that put
a heavy burden on the country parson was the education of
his children. The local church school did very well for the
first few years, but parents felt that they would like their
children to associate too with those who would be their
equals and companions in later life, and this meant sending
them away to boarding schools, with their ever-increasing
fees. The fact that the authorities graded the country parishes
considerably lower than those of town and industrial
parishes, shows that they too believed that it was cheaper to
live in the country. One clergyman told me — and he was a
member of the Patronage Board — that, of course, we could
live cheaper, because there was no need for us to buy meat,
we could live on rabbits. I was quite fond of rabbit pie, and
in my young days enjoyed many a leveret I had shot, but I
have never tasted rabbit from that day to this! It is not a nice
picture, is it? But possibly such gossipy bits will make the
most appeal in years to come. These pages describe the
teething troubles of an early phase in the career of the
diocese as I got to know it.

Before I move on to speak of my first preferment, I must

finish with this early period. This section has given me more trouble than all the previous pages put together, for in reading it over — after a few days — I began to wonder whether I had given the reader here and there a wrong impression, and whether in other parts I had been guilty of exaggeration. The result was that much of it was re-written, softening it here and cushioning it there. In reading it over again after the lapse of a similar period, I felt I had been unduly sensitive and had used too many cushions. Once again it was re-written — and nearer to the original.

I have to be more or less content with the description I have given of some of the difficulties that faced the new diocese as it started on its career — physical difficulties of shape and extent, difficulties bound up with its dual character, as partly industrial and populous, and partly agricultural and thinly populated — and the reaction these factors had on the minds of the clergy. However, I must say that it outgrew and surmounted them all, and achieved a unity on a higher level, in the realm of the spirit and the affections, acquiring, and manifesting, that warm loyal sentiment that we associate with the home. It became a very devoted and a very happy diocese. As one who worked in it for forty years and under all its bishops, I am happy to bear this testimony to it.

It has been fortunate in all its bishops, men of differing gifts and parts which they put unreservedly at the disposal of the diocese. We country clergy had a firm and understanding friend in our first Bishop, that approachable, human, friendly, breezy character, Bishop Bevan. I shall not presume to say where I think each of them excelled — simply to say this, that I was happy under them all. Some of the clergy went in fear of Bishop Morgan, and with very good reason if they were slovenly in their attire and personal appearance, and especially if they were slipshod in their conduct of the services.

EIGHT

My First Benefice – Mid-Wales

<hr/>

ABOUT SIX MONTHS after my interview with the bishop, a letter arrived one morning offering me the living of Llanfihangel Rhydithon, which was certainly in the hill-country, for it took in a considerable portion of the Radnor Forest. As I still considered myself capable of tackling any of the bigger parishes in the diocese, it did not go down very well. I wanted work; I was now in my middle thirties and these were the years in which I could do my best work. I was not going alone, I had a partner who was coming with me, as well as the two children, so my wife naturally had to be consulted. We got hold of a map and a railway guide, for the Swansea and Shrewsbury line ran through the parish. We consulted one or two clergymen already there whom we knew. They spoke well of it, that 'as a country parish' it was one of the most 'desirable' in Radnorshire, with a very nice Vicarage, only five minutes from the above main railway line. We began to warm up to the idea. The fact that it was on the main line to Manchester appealed to my wife, and the further fact that it was only a few minutes run from that famous mid-Wales spa, Llandrindod Wells, had also its own attractions, amongst them the fact that it was the venue of the meetings of the Governing Body of the Church in Wales. As parents we could not be oblivious of another fact: that in it was situated the County School.

We decided to go and see it, and the day we chose was one of the wettest days I have ever known, the rain was coming down in torrents and a thin mist covered the top of the hills. We passed the famous Penybont common with its numerous mountain ponies. We saw nothing else until we arrived in front of the church — we were also in front of the little village school, and dozens of little faces could be seen on their feet beside their desks looking at us. Instantly, the infants' teacher, Miss Davies, came out to greet us, and to send word by one of the children to her brother-in-law — one of the wardens, and an old retired school master. He showed us the church and the Vicarage and we liked both — my wife having mostly the Vicarage in mind, and I the church. There was nothing we disliked, unless it was the utter emptiness of the surrounding countryside. The result was that we accepted it. Congratulations began to arrive, one or two of them containing dark hints about Radnorshire people — they had been told that amongst other things they took a lot of understanding, that you could never get near to them.

Later on I discovered how I got the appointment — a discovery calculated to bring more humiliation upon my head, and further to injure my personal pride, for it seems that it came my way not because of any fitness, suitability or qualification in me at all, nor because of my experience, capabilities or approved character, or manner of life, but simply because of one qualification my wife possessed, which seemed the all-important requirement the parish, according to its representatives, was most in need of.

The two representatives at this meeting of the Patronage Board when the appointment was made were the two churchwardens whom I got to know later very well, and had the greatest respect for. And as I knew them so well I am sure they must have asked themselves what the world was coming to, when they, two ordinary country folk, who knew no clergyman except their own and possibly one or two more who had preached at the harvest festival, were cited to attend this meeting which was to appoint a parish priest for their church — mine was the first appointment to the parish according to the new constitution. They could not have been more astonished and surprised than if they were told the following week that Lord Ormathwaite was going to invite two clergymen to help him and his staff appoint a new tenant for one of his farms. Surely the church knew its own clergy: what training they had had, what academic qualifications they possessed, what reputation they bore for earnestness and devotion in their work, and knew too the character and requirements of such a parish as theirs. However, they attended the meeting, but they said not a word. In the end they were asked what they thought of me — did they not think I would suit the parish? What the dickens was all that to them? As long as I was a priest capable of performing my priestly duties in the parish, they had no further interest in me. I could be young or old, fat or lean, as far as they were interested in me, so they dismissed me from their minds, if I had been in their minds at all! What bothered them in the parish was the difficulty of getting somebody to play the organ, and the only question they asked was, could his wife play the organ. The Archdeacon — who told me the story — assured them that she could. That settled it. She got the appointment — and I of course, as a sort of lapdog got in with her, and would do as the Vicar of the parish. I often teased my wife that she got me my first preferment!

At my Institution the church was full and the service impressed me very much — almost as much as my Ordination, for then I was merely received into one of the Orders of the church, now I was put in actual, spiritual, charge of all the people of the parish — their pastor and shepherd. A responsibility was laid upon me that I could not share with anyone else. It was a very solemn occasion and the service was such as to emphasise it. I have often wondered since whether some form of public recognition or welcome could not be devised for the coming to the parish of a new curate. It would be too much to ask the Bishop to conduct these public welcomes or minor institutions, but it could be conducted by the Rural Dean, or even by the Vicar himself. It would certainly add importance and dignity to the post, and give the new arrival an immediate status and an official recognition — just at the time he can do with it. As it is now, his arrival means no more than the arrival of the morning paper or the milk. He just arrives at his lodgings and proceeds the following Sunday to preach his first sermon. On the way home it might occur to some member to remark to another: 'So that's our new curate'.

As I said, my Institution was a memorable occasion to me.

Part of the ceremony, or procedure, was the ringing of the church bell, to indicate to the parishioners that their new pastor had arrived and had taken possession of the church. Much attention is always paid by the parishioners to the number of tolls the new incumbent gives to the bell, for it is an indication to them of the number of years he means to stay amongst them, and a lot of clergy like to yield to the curiosity of the people. I rang it seven times: not that I expected to be there for seven years, for the Bishop had assured me that after four years or so, I should be brought back to the industrial part of the diocese, an assurance that pleased me very much, as it implied a belief that I was capable of filling one of those larger parishes, and that it would not be to the advantage of the diocese if I was kept out here longer than four years. On the way back to the Vicarage from the service, in the Bishop's car, he told me that I would find that Radnorshire people will go a long way in a long time. Here it was again: *Radnorshire people*; I was really now beginning to wonder what sort of people I had come amongst. I had already heard that they were difficult to understand, difficult to get near to, and now in addition they could be stubborn as well, for they would not be driven except at their own chosen pace.

For the first few months, we were trying to fill the Vicarage, for it had seven bedrooms, a study, drawing room, dining room, hall, kitchen, an equally large back kitchen where the boiler was and where the washing was done, an ordinary pantry and a butler's pantry. It had a huge coal house capable of storing ten or twelve tons of coal. Underneath was a huge cellar, including a wine cellar whose walls were lined with shelves. We went at this job merrily — were we not jumping from a curate's mere £180 to close on £350! We got new dining room and drawing room suites, two bedroom suites and a new piano. Fortunately for us, at this time, there were weekly sales of furniture in Llandrindod Wells, because the depression had already begun to hit this famous spa whose prosperity had been in a large measure built up on the money of the industrialists and business people of South Wales. The stable we did not pretend to fill, so its saddle-room, two stalls and loose-box remained empty, so did the coachhouse and the cow-shed, though to our surprise all of them got filled with something in the course of the years. It had a tennis court, and at the back a small field, called in Radnorshire a plock. Altogether it was a very nice vicarage, and my wife and I and the children spent nine happy years in it — much too large, but a wonderful place for the children to grow up in. It had its drawbacks of course, for it involved, for one thing, the filling and trimming of ten lamps every day, including the wall lamps, but then we had a maid and all this work did not fall on my wife.

While I am at it, it is best to say here all that has to be said about the house. The winters in Radnorshire could be very long and very severe. We had one or two of them there in my time, but in ordinary winters, I often had to go through the trap-door leading to the water tank just under the ceiling, with a hammer to cut up the ice, and a candle to run along the pipes to thaw them. It was a very cramped position and could only be accomplished on one's stomach. One did not grumble about this, one accepted it as part of a severe winter in the country.

Later on in the spring I had to tackle another problem: how to get rid of jackdaws from our chimneys, for they began working and 'jacking' soon after four o'clock and waking the children up, indeed, waking up the whole household. Every spring, for about four years, for I was fighting a most determined enemy, I got up soon after four o'clock and went out to the stable with my gun, and from there, opening the door just sufficiently to push the barrel through, I shot at them as they alighted on the chimney pots. I must have got at least half a dozen every year. We fixed 'roses' on the pots to prevent their getting in, yet despite all this one or two managed to get through to raise a new brood. I was astonished at the power they had in their beaks, for they managed to pull apart wires of quite considerable thickness and push through. And though they were in deadly fear of me and the gun, yet it took me four years before I finally got rid of them.

Near the Vicarage there was a clump of trees with two owls in it. I like owls, I like their call at nights, for to me it makes the night much more silent, and eerie. They were part of the night orchestra that lulled me to sleep as a child, supported by the barking of the dogs — their howling on moonlit nights — occasionally the short yaps of the fox, accompanied by the wind in the tall trees that ringed the farmhouse.

But one morning, very early, I caught an owl taking out of a song-bird's nest the young of a day old. Out came the gun again and there were no more owls about the Vicarage. It grieved me to have to do this, but to me, a countryman, came first the song birds.

As to my recreations, I had two: walking and fishing. I thought nothing of walking thirty miles or so a day; when I wanted to go farther afield I took out my bicycle. Many of my walks were over the Radnor Forest, until I got to know most of its main paths, gullies and ponds. I liked the Radnor Forest. I listened to tales of its tragedies, its feuds and its legends, and wrote them up, principally, for our national daily, the *Western Mail*. Children who wouldn't go to sleep were warned that if they didn't, Silver John would come round and take them away. Deep in its fastnesses dwelt the dragon. I often spoke to an old man who lived up on the slopes of the Forest and who maintained that though he had never seen it he had heard it breathing. Was it because of the dragon that our Christian ancestors ringed it round with St Michael churches, one of which was my own church of Llanfihangel Rhydithon?

I have spoken of tragedies — this, though it happened over two hundred years ago, is still remembered: In the churchyard of Llanfihangel Rhydithon there is a gravestone bearing the following inscription: 'Here lieth the bodies of John and Thomas Chandlour.... also the body of Edward Chandlour.... John, Thomas, Edward, died Feb. 13, 1767, aged 34, 30, 24.

While shepherd's watch their flocks by night
Where as by chance did wee
Then it did please Almighty God
To call upon us three.
Then underneath the milk-white snow
Our bodies there they lay
Until our dearest friends did know
To bear us safe away.

This stone was erected to replace an old one (which by the way is still there, resting against the yew tree) which bore the above inscription '..... 1898.'

The families living at the foot of the Forest are not going to let this tragedy be forgotten, for it contains the warning that no person may expect pity from the Forest when it rages in its fury.

It seems the first of the three went up to try to bring the sheep down to safety, but failed to return, the second went up to look for him and he never returned either. This, one would think would be sufficient to demand caution, but another was found still brave enough to defy the anger of the Forest, with the inevitable result.

I also made some research into the why and when of the decay of Welsh in Radnorshire, and discovered some interesting facts; amongst them the fact that Radnorshire people did not let their language die as if it was a matter of no interest or importance to them, as is generally assumed. Oh, yes, there were last ditchers amongst them, as the history of some of the chapels testifies.

There was no golf immediately available, as to my brethren in the South, so, to establish an equitable balance between us, I turned to fishing, and enjoyed many hours every week on the river bank. Not that I caught many fish, but I enjoyed it all: where the peace was equal to the beauty and where the stillness revealed how quietly nature works. I had a friend here who saved me many hours, if not many days of useless casting on the river: the local grocer, who had grown up on the river bank, and who knew the fish as well as he knew his customers. On a doubtful day I always called in the shop to get his opinion; he would come out, lift his eyes up to the sky and turn round to view it in every quarter, at the same time sniffing as it were the air to get a *taste* of the wind as well as its direction; then he would turn to me and say: 'Vicar, you can go home' or 'You ought to catch a few today'. Sometimes, I would disregard his advice only to return home disappointed. Fishing and walking were my main recreations and interests, apart from reading which continued to be a passion with me: a passion noticed in very early years by my parents, which convinced them, that enslaved by it to such a degree, no power on earth could make a farmer of me, and if it could, it would not be worth it.

Even in such a small parish with only one church, there was some work to do. The visiting of my eighteen or so church families did not constitute *work* for me at all, for I was so often in different parts of the parish on one of my walks that I took advantage of the occasion to call on the homes that I passed.

My Sunday duties involved the taking of two services and the preaching of two sermons, with an early communion on the first Sunday in the month. I am not one who believes in making any work more difficult or more laborious than one need, but I prepared most of my sermons with the care that I would were I to preach them in Westminster Abbey, noting very carefully all the quotations — and often slipping across to the church to try them out before an imaginary congregation. I have always believed that preaching is important, that it will always be important — this exercising of the power of the word, by which the apostolic church made such a shattering and effective onslaught on the ancient world. But I have lived to see — and that in the country of great preachers and great preaching — the sermon declining and shrinking to be merely incidental in the course of the service, for which is devoted eight to twelve minutes — hardly daring to make it fifteen minutes — of light, chatty talk, giving as the excuse that present-day congregations cannot understand New Testament vocabulary nor comprehend its simple teaching.

The morning celebrations were plainly rendered, but as time went on I introduced a little more music, and on Sunday evenings just before the blessing, I held a sort of choir — or congregational — practice, to extend the range of our hymns, especially those for the special seasons of the church and for saints' days.

I had it just before the blessing so that nobody could leave the church under the excuse that the service was over. Indeed, nobody attempted to, for these practices were very much liked — people liked singing hymns, and I think they appreciated, too, my evident consideration for them in having them on Sunday evenings when they were all dressed up and all in their places. It is not always sufficiently realised by clergy what an extra amount of work it entails to wash and change and get ready for an evening's choir practice after a long and heavy day's labour.

There was a cross on the altar and two candlesticks with candles in, but they had never been lit — light coming from two wall-lamps on each side. One of the lamps obligingly got out of order, so it gave me an excuse not to light the other, but as I had to get light in the sanctuary, I lit the candles instead. Nobody commented on the fact. It may be that they rather liked them lit and may have wondered why they had not been lit before. Candles are for lighting. I had plenty of excuse to light them in the evenings; after a time I lit them also in the mornings — without excuse! Again no comment — a typical Radnorshire attitude. But then nobody could object to candles being lit to give light.

As to my own personal life, I made at the very commencement three or four rules, drawn up in fear, and to be observed with the utmost diligence, as I recalled instances of what havoc long years in the country had wrought in some lives, of which I felt sure Radnorshire, too, could provide examples: men grown bitter by long neglect, men living in isolation, lacking the society of fellow priests, deprived of the encouragement and inspiration that comes from such inter-course and the exchange of ideas and experiences, men who might have been saved had they had in the course of those long, long years one visit from their Father in God; men who had in the end become, in their thinking and living, indistinguishable from the labourers and farm servants who made up the majority of their congregation, having aband-oned all intellectual pursuits, men having almost forgotten they were priests. Such tragedies were not many, but they were known. They might have been saved. In the quarterly lists of Bishops' engagements one looked in vain for some such entry as this: 'A day with the Rev. John Jones and his family, Llanunig Vicarage, (Dedication St Solitaire) Frontier Pass, Outer Cambria'. Such cases of course do not happen today, and that for many reasons: long incumbencies are no longer in the fashion, scarcity of priests has made changes easier, if not inevitable, the grouping of parishes, the formation of Rectorial parishes and the appearance of the cheap motor car — the early Fords and the Austin Sevens. I am now of course speaking of the 'twenties and though a few clergy possessed cars at this time, many of us country clergy who were in the lower income group had to wait many years yet. I knew one country clergyman who had bought his car for £15, and strange to say it would go, if only perhaps like Crawshaw-Bailey's engine:

Which according to her power
She could go five miles an hour,
All a-puffin and a-blowin,
All a-chuggin and a-roarin!

One rule, to save me from degenerating into a slow, ambling rustic, concerned my reading, another concerned my private devotions, lest I should too often forget I was a priest. As part of my devotions I read every morning one chapter of the New Testament in Greek and in the Vulgate, from a polyglot Bible. Just before breakfast, we had family prayers. One of the manuals I used was that drawn up by Bishop Owen of St David's. This we kept up for many years, but eventually it died, or rather had to be discontinued, for a very unexpected reason: When our two girls started at the County School, they had a train to catch, and one would rush in, shouting at the door before she knew prayers had begun: 'Mummie, I can't find my Geography Book'. There was such a lot of rushing about, such a lot of searching for hats, hockey sticks, or coats that couldn't be found, and a final stampede before the last Amen had had time to die away, to continue the search, that I decided to discontinue them in case the children began to look upon them as a nuisance. I was sorry it came to this, for I was rather proud of myself, as a *pater familias*, gathering my family round me — we had a maid as well — every morning; and in asking for their protection during the day, I surely could not help impressing upon them, especially my children, that I cared very much for them — more than they might at times imagine. On a lower level, it enlarged one's area of possession, which, to a simple mind, who had not much property to boast of, could not help giving much satisfaction to the *ego*, and in contemplation bring a pleasant feeling of importance to a personality that could at times do with a little boosting.

It may have been a silly thing to do, but as I have said, I often prepared my sermons with all the care that I would devote to them were they to be preached in Westminster Abbey — it gave me much satisfaction, and served constantly to remind me that there were higher standards of sermon-making and preaching than might be called for in a small country church like mine. It however, saved one from falling into the slack and reprehensible habit of satisfying myself with some such remark as: 'it will have to do this morning' or 'they don't appreciate good sermons'.

I attended all clerical meetings and conferences, and blessed the opportunities of twice a year attending the meetings of the Governing Body of the church, meeting a few acquaintances and making a few new ones. We had our Chapter meetings, and we formed study groups, for younger clergy were now beginning to appear in these country parishes, until in time the majority of them were filled with young men; the older men still sitting tight down in the industrial and town parishes. But, gradually, some of the problems of this geographically awkward diocese, so sharply split into two sections of the most diverse character, were beginning to iron themselves out.

To return to the Governing Body meetings, which we so eagerly looked forward to. It was difficult at first for a poor clergyman to know what to make of it all, with its Rolls-Royces and flashy cars weaving in and out of the crowd, each with its liveried chauffeur. Was it a Board meeting of some gigantic industrial concern, with nation-wide ramifications? In these limousines sat lords and ladies, country gentry and high executives, from all parts of Wales. No less conspicuous were the stringed hats of the Bishops, the gaitered legs of the upper hierarchy, and the numerous rosettes of the Canons and the Rural Deans. Truly the Church in Wales was on show, yet to a Welsh-speaking priest it all seemed so alien, and remote, and he felt that if this was the church, he could not count in it more than one of the buttons on the Archbishop's gaiters. There were significant gaps — one looked in vain for the man with the blue veins in his hands and his face; absent also were the men in breeches and leggings whom one met in the marts and the fairs of the market towns of Wales.

Of course a great change has come over the Governing Body in the last fifty years, it now looks much more democratic and uniform. The Bishops and all the higher clergy have discarded their breeches and gaiters. With the help of Burtons, C & A, Hodges and many others, the lay members are so well dressed, and dressed so much alike, that one cannot tell the squire from the professional, or the factory-floor man, unless one is near enough to catch the accent. I wondered what impression it made on the Radnor-shire native who worshipped on Sunday in a plain and secluded Bethel, or, for that matter, what impression it would make on a similar country congregation out in Welsh Wales! However, may one poor clergyman speak on behalf of himself and his family? — these laymen of the business and financial world looked after our interests with genuine personal care, and husbanded the then tight and inadequate assets and resources of the church with a conscientious concern for our welfare, that, gradually, by this expertise and 'know how', they lifted us out of our domestic worries and constant strain. I would like to pay my humble tribute to them, and especially to Mr David Vaughan, who in the last decade or so has, with his trained and canny wizardry, put one part of the church's house at any rate in very good order.

One listened for a word or two in Welsh, but none came. As seen at the Governing Body meetings, so 'Anglican' did our church still appear. The attitude of the first Archbishop (Dr Alfred George Edwards) was well known to us. He did not value highly the use and survival of the Welsh tongue, and yet only a gap of one generation — that of his father — stood between him and the Welsh-speaking peasantry of Cardigan-shire. His brother, Henry Thomas Edwards (1837-1884), Dean of Bangor, was, on the other hand, a man deeply concerned with the claims of the Welsh people, the Welsh church and the Welsh language. There was of course plenty of Welsh to be heard in the hotels and boarding houses, on the streets and round corners, as two clergymen bumped into each other: 'Jew, Jew, Dai Bachan, 'dw i ddim wedi dy weld di ...' ('Jew, Jew, Dai, man, I haven't seen you since we came down from Coll').

Very soon after my arrival I started on my work. I would bring to bear on it my very considerable experience garnered in big parishes. I had plenty of ideas and plans and I was determined to implement them with a resolute will. My predecessor was an elderly man who had spent the whole of his long life in small country parishes. What had he seen! I would show them! But, before very long, I discovered that my predecessor and the country clergy generally had run their parishes in the only way they could be run in those days. They could undoubtedly have done more for the young people, but the young people were not then the problem they later became — they were still in the churches, in the congregations and in the Sunday schools. It was only after the First World War that the churches realised that if they were to keep the interest and retain the membership of these young people they would have to devise some means of focussing their interest and absorbing their energy. I was in the country long enough to have a great admiration for the older clergy. Not all my ideas fell through. There was in the parish a branch of the Mothers' Union which my wife took over and ran very successfully. We started a series of regular meetings for the young girls of the church, to bring together once a fortnight this young element in the church and give them the opportunity, which they did not often have in a scattered parish such as ours, of meeting one another in a free and happy atmosphere. It could not help but strengthen their ties with, and their loyalty to, the church. My wife naturally had a great part to play in this effort, and between us we served in this way the needs of these young people and of the church.

I began also to organize a series of similar meetings for the young men and youths of the parish, meeting as in the case of the girls, once a fortnight. This too proved quite a flourishing concern. In time the Bishop (Bevan) who was then the president of the C.E.M.S. got to hear about it, and at his suggestion I turned it into a branch of the Church of England Men's Society, and strange to say, from that moment it began to flag. I can offer no explanation for it, I merely state the fact. Sometime later I listened to a country programme on the radio in which a Shropshire clergyman said that country people don't like to be organized, that to do so would stifle the effort, but 'to give the organization a name was to kill it'. Those were his exact words. I often thought about them afterwards.

My wife and I shared the work of the Sunday school on Sunday afternoons, which was very faithfully attended. In writing these reminiscences I am conscious of her loss, for she had such a good memory.

In this way we worked on, quietly, for nine years. The four, which the Bishop said would be the extent of our stay, had long gone by. Indeed, a new bishop had come who could not be expected to know of his predecessor's promises, and in any case would not feel bound to carry them out.

Looking back through the register, I find that I did not rush to make the great changes I had visualized. It took me two years before I introduced an early celebration every Sunday, in addition to the one on the first Sunday of the month. I did that as much for myself as for the congregation. When I came to the parish there was no collection at any morning service except that at the eleven o'clock communion on the first Sunday in the month. I introduced them at every morning service, but did not do so at the early celebrations, nor at the celebrations on Saints' days. I find that the collections for my first full year (1927-1928) amounted to £23.13.0, and in my last full year, to £24.0.2. These included all the special collections as well, for example, for the missionary societies and hospitals, etc. I am quite proud to think that in my nine years in the parish, the collections increased by seven shillings and twopence, for they were the years of depression. My people felt the stress of the times very acutely, for they were upland farmers who relied largely on sheep which they grazed on the Forest during the summer months. Many a time I've seen them driving their flock past the Vicarage in the morning, making for the Penybont mart, and driving them back again in the evening. One family which had emigrated to America some years previously, returned to the parish to see if things were

better in the old country. It was after the 1929 Wall Street
collapse, but back they went after a few months, finding that
prospects were not much brighter here, though we had not to
sell our lambs at a shilling each as they had had to do in
America.

Our churchyard was a very small one, and I didn't like to
think we were disturbing and exposing so many bones each
time we had a burial, though that had been done at all
churchyards along the centuries. We were given the plot of
ground and I was able to find enough money to fence it in
with a dwarf wall, on which were imbedded iron railings. It
was consecrated on 25 August 1931, by Bishop Bevan.

The Vicar's fee for taking a burial when I arrived there was
one shilling! The church had by then issued a new schedule
of fees, but as the burials were so few, I suppose, the old
Vicar hadn't bothered about it. How long this had been the
standard fee I don't know, possibly from medieval times. As
a man who rejoiced in all sorts of survivals, I was happy to
think that in this small matter, I stood, possibly the last, in a
long line of parish priests, back to, and beyond, the
Reformation.

During the whole of my incumbency I took only seven
weddings which meant that before each one I had to spend
the previous evening in familiarising myself with the service
once again, for one can forget a lot in twelve or eighteen
months, and I was always a stickler for doing things properly
and in order.

With regard to baptism there was not the same anxiety —
as the service was simpler, and as I had twenty-three in that
time, it meant that I had been able to keep my hand in. As
for burials, of which I had about the same number
(twenty-one), the service was simpler still, and apart from
watching that the 90th psalm was not used for a minor, there
was little that could go wrong.

I must say something here, as I have promised, about
Radnorshire people. I had of course long learnt by now the
truth of the Bishop's words that they would go a long way in
a long time, and I was already pursuing my work in the full
acceptance of that basic fact. Some of my early experiences
will best describe the sort of people they are, or at any rate,

were: My first harvest festival was a disaster. Where, usually on such occasions, one gets a packed church, ours had only little more than the normal attendance. Some days later I asked my churchwarden — a farmer — what had happened. 'Well,' he said, 'you put it on the same day as the great annual sheep sale at Knighton'. I said, 'Why didn't you tell me then?' His reply was: 'You didn't ask me'. That, I think, tells a lot about them — they mind their own business and keep their mouths shut. He told me also that I had put it on a night when there was no moon. That, I must admit, I could have thought of, for a moonlit night is an important matter to people who have to walk unlit roads and paths. If they had a Vicar who was prepared to ignore the annual sheep sale at Knighton, and in addition the shining quarter of the moon, let him get on with it! Once, I learnt from our eldest girl that I had put my concert on the same day as the long-established quarterly meetings of one of the chapels, so had one of the lads blurted out to her. Fortunately for me there was ample time for me to alter the date, and so prevent a clash that I would not like to happen at any cost. I don't think any of my people would have told me — if the Vicar wants to do things like that, well, that's his business. I was saved by this young boy who was not yet a fully-grown Radnorshire man, and had not learnt to keep his mouth shut, but from what I heard afterwards, the 'talk' his father gave him when he discovered what had happened, would ensure that he would not interfere or meddle again in what did not concern him! And this was another Radnorshire man in the making. I never knew a people who just minded their own business to such an extent. Some have seen behind it all a border people, long harried by raids from one side or the other of Offa's Dyke, and who had learnt along the centuries to be cautious and to be spare of words. I got to know them well and got to like them; and when the time came for me to leave them, it was a sad and sorry priest that parted with them after those nine years. The many expressions of sorrow, and the valuable tokens of appreciation, which we received at that time showed that they were equally sorry to part with me and my family. They had really taken us to their hearts, and when our boy was born, such was the interest that he might have been a child of royalty: was he not, as they reminded us, the first boy to be born at the Vicarage. Long may our Vicarages enjoy the interest and the affection of the parishioners.

Had Radnorshire people developed into a type of their own, it ought not to surprise one, for they had been cut off from contact with Welsh thought, aspirations and culture by the barrier of language for two hundred years. They, again, were not English people: the only thing they had derived from England was the language. I found them to be what one would expect them to be, had one not heard those dark hints and enigmatic references, just Welsh people who had unfortunately lost their historic language as it was gradually forced west by the advance of the English.

Apart from that, they were the sons and daughters of Wales, living in a part of the country which by its place-names and personal names testified to that fact. They shared the same history, the same pattern of religion, the same educational system, from the primary up to University level.

There has been and there still is much discussion as to what is the best type of man to send to a country parish. He should, for his own sake, have some country interests, a liking for long walks and if he is interested in birds and their habits all the better. I spent many hours up on the Radnor Forest watching the black-headed gulls which came out to breed in a big pool there, and I took part in a radio programme to find out which was the first bird to pipe up in the morning. I have long lost my notes, but I think it was the song-thrush. He can spend hours talking to old inhabitants about ghosts, apparitions, fairies, legends, untoward incidents and gone-by customs, not forgetting the fishing, which can account for many days when one has not too much to do. The possibilities and opportunities are endless. If a clergyman has no interest at all in these hobbies and kindred pursuits, he should have an unquenchable thirst for reading. I know of no other compensating alternative. Some insist that the country clergyman should, as he now belongs to a farming community, be himself a son of the farm so that he can on his visits to the farms move knowledgeably round the folds and the fields without making blunders as between breeds, to say nothing of species. I don't think this is essential at all. As a farmer's son, I could move intelligently, even learnedly, amongst the stock, the crops and the implements. I knew a good horse from an indifferent one; I knew all their blemishes and their good points. It is true the Hereford breed was new to me, but after my warden had initiated me into their good points, I felt I had a working knowledge of them. But I deliberately refrained from airing my knowledge as I accompanied my farmer members around the farms. I deemed it the proper attitude to adopt, which I was sure was also psychologically sound, to say as little as I could, beyond taking due interest in what was told me and shown me. Hang it all! they listened to me talking twice a Sunday, and occasionally perhaps talking over their heads, especially in those sermons prepared for Westminster Abbey! It would be intolerable if I invaded the farm and again talked learnedly about stock and crops, depriving them of the one province where *they* could talk to *me* and teach *me* something. It was more than a self-respecting man could be expected to put up with! So I held my tongue and listened. No, I don't think it is a disadvantage in a townsman, in his work as a country priest, as long as he has a liking for the quiet, unhurried ways of nature and the seasons; indeed, it is to his advantage if farmyard ignorance compels him to leave a small foothold to the farmer where he can stand up to him and do the talking for once.

I never found any difficulty in breaking through the natural reserve of the country cottager and getting him to talk — there was always his garden in which I invariably found something to admire. I would come away having been told the real secret of growing certain vegetables, and often with a specimen from the particular vegetable I had most admired. Nor did I find it difficult either to get the young lads and farm servants, naturally shy and reserved with strangers, to talk. One only needs to remember their interest in bird and wild life around them, and there will occur plenty of openings where one can break through. Often, specimens of wild life may be seen as pets in many families — in one farm I saw two young buzzards which were being hand-reared. Simply to give the young boys the opportunity of telling me how they caught them was to set them going, even to the extent of wanting to take me to the woods to show me the nests of some of our rarer birds, such as the heron. Badgers, though plentiful are not often seen, and are therefore a source of curiosity to country lads. Not only was I told they could show me a sett, but I got out of them the manner in which they were caught. It is a cruel sport to both dog and badger. Dogs are sent into the sett where a life and death struggle ensues, in which the dogs are often driven back to the mouth of the hole, but if in his anger and fear the badger chases the dogs just a few inches beyond, there is a man above it with a long-handled tongs made by the blacksmith ready to clamp it round his neck and secure him. In fact there survives much thoughtless cruelty in the countryside.

Country people are not irreverent but few country congregations kneel during prayers. Well into the last century the floors of many of our country churches were made of mould and clay, which in earlier times were spread with a good covering of rushes. These, when the congregation was thin, could be gathered into a heap to make quite a comfortable hassock for the kneeler, but it must have been at all times a *painful* problem, for the knees were never intended to hold up the body long. In my native parish the local historian says that the worshippers solved the problem by taking with them a coarse kind of rug. The puritans objected to kneeling as to much else, and when the denominations began to spread in the country it is no wonder that the practice, having anatomical advantages to commend it, should become the accepted habit. But I blame the introduction of the pew for this as much as anything, for it made leaning forward on the pew in front so much like kneeling that nobody could tell the difference unless one went there to examine the matter. I certainly believed — and taught — that good Anglicans, who had inherited the right way, should offer their prayers on their knees, but my people persisted in thinking differently. Today it is conceded that prayers may be offered in any posture, certainly that no position involving discomfort can add anything to an act of worship. Psychology, long before it had a name, must have had much to do with our posture in prayer, for in standing up one is adopting an attitude of equality with the one faced, possibly boldness, or defiance, whereas in kneeling a feeling of humbleness and unworthiness is induced, surely the only attitude befitting a creature before his creator.

NINE

Remembering Radnorshire

————————◁▷————————

ON ONE OCCASION I went to preach at a neighbouring church and unfortunately picked up a bad habit from the curate-in-charge there. I noticed that after the service was over he put down in the register the number present — there was a column provided for it. It seemed to me a very good idea, and I decided that I would adopt it, though there was no such column in my register. Pleased by my interest, he turned back the pages to show how it had worked for the previous twelve months or so. I noticed that on quite a number of Sundays his congregation was very small, but he was a resourceful man, and had added 'a rainy day'; when it dropped to a lower figure, 'a very wet and rainy day'; when it fell lower still he was not worried, for the explanation was forthcoming: 'torrential rain and floods', and when his congregation was nearly wiped out, he was still unperturbed, for opposite the figure of four or five there were the words 'snow', or 'heavy snow'.

The following Sunday I started, but one problem faced me at the commencement: I was not good at all at staring at the congregation, after the manner of some. Readers of a previous chapter will know that I have spoken on this matter before, and declared how very much I envied those clergy who, immediately they got into the pulpit, began boldly, defiantly, to stare out their congregation, pew by pew, until they had established as it were an understanding with them that for the next half hour or so they were to sit quietly in their pews and listen to him, and not to question anything that he said, or indulge in any other nonsense. But I had to try and count my people somehow; the best opportunity I found was during the singing of the hymns. As many of the verses were well known to me, I could, while singing one verse, make furtive glances down one aisle, and up the next aisle while singing another verse. Though it was difficult, I felt sure that I was always correct to within one or two. As ill-luck would have it, my congregation on the day I started counting must have been an exceptionally good one, for from that day it began to dwindle, and hardly ever did I return home on Sunday a happy man. To account for the drop in number — small at first — I began to count children. I was already playing with my native honesty, but it was nothing compared with what I did before the end! I even counted as present farmers that I knew would be there but for the fact that a case of difficult calving had to happen on a Sunday; others I counted, and with an easy conscience — too easy — for I knew they would be present but for the fact that they had visitors, had a bad cold, or were in bed with the flu. With many subterfuges of this kind I managed to keep something like an average congregation in existence. But soon things got worse, and sad to say, as it dropped, lower and lower did I stoop to account for it. I had soon to bring in 'rain', 'more rain', 'tempests' and 'floods'. I was conscious that I was trifling with my native honesty and doing a great wrong to my better self. But what could I do, I could not let my congregation vanish like this. Things got worse still so that I had to call to my aid 'snow', 'more snow', 'drifts', 'higher drifts' even 'hedge-high drifts'. I was almost beside myself: I could not get rain heavy enough, floods extensive enough, nor drifts high enough to account for the disappearance of my congregation.

What I have said here is perfectly true, and I say it as it may save another young man from adopting so foolish a practice. I ought to have remembered how David brought down upon himself (I Chronicles, 21, 1-14) the displeasure of the Almighty for counting the people. Anyhow before the congregation completely vanished and I had to close the doors of the church, I gave the practice up, and strange to say, from that very day my congregation began to improve, until in a very short time, I was again a happy man officiating to an average congregation.

My congregation must have fluctuated at times as all congregations do, but whether a bad stretch of low attendance happened to coincide with this new experiment I cannot now be sure. Perhaps the whole thing happened only in my mind, for fear begets what it fears, and shows it under a magnifying glass.

I liked to talk to the older generation about old customs, old ways, and old superstitions, and to ask them whether they had in their possession old account books, old letters or old books. In this way I came across a book — not old, but rare — written by the Rev. William Seaton, Rector of Lampeter Velfrey, Pembrokeshire, bearing the title, *Heirs of Promise; or the Church in the Wilderness,* and published in 1834. As so little was known of him, some interesting correspondence followed (see the *Llan* for October 1932). As it was written by a clergyman of the diocese of St David's, I sent it to the Bishop for the Diocesan library, but that was before I had personal knowledge of the work of the National Library and the services it renders to readers and research workers. Has a catalogue of the contents of these diocesan libraries ever been published for the benefit of historians and readers? Surely it would meet with the approval of the Church in Wales if that were done, and very likely, ready approval for their transfer to the National Library.

Amongst my occupations was that of keeping the grounds in good order and doing the garden, and here I came across a weed that I had never encountered before — one called horse's tail, a long elastic, string-like growth which throws its roots so very deep that it is impossible almost to eradicate it.

I kept also the tennis lawn in good order, because I wanted the children to learn to play. We had brought with us all the croquet mallets and irons from my wife's home where at one time we had played so many games. When friends and visitors came, there were therefore invariably games of tennis and croquet.

Many of our neighbours were folks considerably older than we were, and my wife looked younger even than her years. When I introduced her at our first bazaar to a neighbour, he just exploded: 'This chit of a girl'. Our nearest neighbour was a priest of the old order; he would not attend except strictly church meetings, such as chapter meetings, ruridecanal and diocesan conferences. All the others he haughtily dismissed as abetting the new doctrine that salvation was now only attainable by committees. He was a great student and a greater reader, the last thing he did at night was to put ready his Greek and Syriac Bibles for the following morning's reading in both versions. He was a bachelor, and had lived to rue the fact that he did not as a young man get himself a wife. Without a wife these large country vicarages are cold and empty places. It might have also saved him from becoming mean. I was there once when four or five mothers had come to buy apples which he had put out in strips on the bare floor of the unused dining-room or drawing-room, and which he was now selling according to their quality and size. For the smaller ones he charged a penny a pound. I thought what a pity he did not feel it in his heart to give these away to the children of his church, it would have gained him many more friends.

Every Ash Wednesday we had a visit from a clergyman who lived about six miles away and who walked out to have tea with us always on this day. Lent, he said, always made him very miserable, and as I knew him to be a very sincere and devout priest, I can quite understand that small lapses from his strict rules would at this season of self-examination cause him much heart-searching, and indeed misery. We hoped that with the very nice cup of tea my wife made and the cheerful conversation we tried to keep up, we would brace him up to walk the six miles back and face Lent with a little lighter heart.

Another of our neighbours was the sporting parson. As you approached the door, you were met by two gun-dogs who kept up such a din, barking so loud and incessantly that you could not hear the greetings and first bits of conversation as you entered the house. One would think that the dogs would be checked — pets and house-dogs might be, but not gun-dogs, and certainly not by a sportsman such as our neighbour was. In the hall one passed three or four fishing rods, caps and hats decorated with flies, a gun, two shoulder-high, forked walking sticks, wellingtons and waders!

Within the circle of our acquaintance there was a parson and his wife who were always seen out together, and who seemed very happy in each other's company as I am sure they were. But there was one recurring occasion when they disagreed, even to high words, and that was the occasion when the lady went on a shopping expedition, for while he had very definite and fixed ideas as to what was proper and permissible for a parson's wife to wear, she couldn't care less. So, when she paraded herself before him in her new finery, he simply exploded in his vexation and anger: 'You can't wear that, you must take it back first thing in the morning — first thing in the morning. I won't have it, I won't have it at all'. Nothing ever went back. As in the case of most married couples they got to know in time, I suppose, what to expect from each other — and accept it. She knew that whatever she bought her husband would be scandalised by it, and order her — for the sake of the good name of the church and for the ideal of restraint and modesty which should be exercised in all Christian homes and especially in vicarages — to take it back 'first thing in the morning'. He, on his part, knew that when she went on these expeditions his sense of what was decent and proper in the eyes of the church as well as in his own would be outraged. He would, of course, as usual, express his horror at it, however futile and ineffective that had been along the years. He never changed, neither did she, but kept on ignoring both husband and church, consulting only her own personal and independent taste. Happy indeed must be the clerical couple who find only one thing in their life over which they disagree. When I come to think of it, she could turn round and ask how, in the name of conscience could the church talk about propriety in the matter of dress, for was there ever a stage figure dressed up in a more bizarre and comical outfit than a little fat bishop, or archdeacon in a black apron, breeches and gaiters — even though their legs happened to be straight!

I have often wondered what, ultimately, is the fate of archidiaconal and episcopal cast-offs. I have never seen any hanging up in second-hand clothes' shops. Are they burnt like old sermons? As a boy, I remember often seeing in Carmarthen town a clergyman who had broken down mentally, walking about in a bishop's hat and frock-coat. On his feet he had a heavy pair of Welsh clogs, with straw in; one could see the straw because he never laced them up. It is obvious where he got the episcopal garments from.

I know what happened in my case. After about fifteen to twenty years, my wife cut down my frock-coat to the length of a lounge coat, and as such it did service for many years as a study coat.

My clerical hat had a more romantic end. I had long discarded it in favour of the trilby, but I dared not go home without it, for my mother would not have me in anything else. In time, as I wore it only at home, I left it there. After my mother's death, my sister came across it, very carefully — and I am sure very reverently — put it away in a hat-box, and, after the manner of women, asked me in the affirmative: 'you won't wear this hat again, Dan'. I said 'no'.

The next time I saw her was in her new hat. She had turned one side up and the other down, and stuck a big feather on, and I never saw my sister looking smarter in any other hat!

I have already said that I had begun to write. At first, articles about the Radnor Forest, for not only did its untamed and primeval character attract me, but also its legends and tragedies. Another matter that from the very first aroused my curiosity and greatly puzzled me was, how a rural area, like Radnorshire, with its sparse population, and where the opportunities of contact, and the spread of a new tongue were so few — how it so quickly and completely succumbed to the advance of English.

I gave some attention also to the churches and church life of Radnorshire, and in two or three articles to the *Llan,* I described the characteristic towers and the general architecture of these Border churches, their screens — some of them of country-wide fame — and other medieval monuments that have managed to survive, along with a reference to two or three of its more noted clergy. It was impossible for me not to note how Radnorshire Sunday schools ranged themselves along the English rather than the Welsh pattern, in that the children left Sunday school when they left the day-school, whereas in Welsh Wales practically the whole congregation attended, forming classes for all ages, even up to the pensioners.

It was the time when the Oxford Group Movement was attracting much attention, and so in our study circle we took one of the contemporary volumes on the character and the ideas of the movement for our reading and discussion. I think the book was A.J. Russell's *For Sinners Only*. We could not ignore it, for it had already captured a member of an old squire family in the county. Fortunately for those of us who were anxious to keep our reading and studies up to date, and to meet other clergy to discuss contemporary problems and trends in the church and in society, Canon Griffith Thomas had recently come to Llandrindod Wells, in whom we found a kindred and sympathetic spirit, ready to support us in all our efforts, even to taking the lead in such endeavours. We owed much to him, and it was in his study that we met. As he also was a contributor to the pages of the *Llan,* he and I became a great deal more than mere neighbours.

As the Vicarage stood alongside the main road from South Wales, through Brecon, Builth Wells and Llandrindod Wells, to Knighton and the north, many were the folks who called. It was impossible therefore but that I should take an interest in them, in their manner of life, in their state of mind and in their life-story. A lot of those who called in my early years in Radnorshire were old soldiers. They all followed the same routine — they marched up to the door, erect and soldier-like, gave a sharp business-like rap on the door and when it was opened, brought their feet together, clicked their heels, saluted and showed their discharge papers, asking for work or help to keep going until they found it. Across their chests they wore a row of ribbons testifying to the campaigns they had taken part in. As time went on they became fewer and fewer, the clicking of heels ceased, the salute was no longer given and the row of ribbons had disappeared, but the old soldier was still there, only he had at last realised the war was over — and forgotten. Who cared any more about Ypres, Mons or Suvla Bay?

I can imagine him as he rested under the shade of a tree, contemplating his experience since he took to the road, and at last being compelled to accept, though it shattered his pride and self-esteem — and which he should have realised long ago — that the war was over and that the world was no longer interested in it, or in the men who brought us victory in it. Yes, at last accepting it, and as an acknowledgement of his folly in not realising it before, ripping off his row of medals and throwing it into the ditch beside him, getting up a much saner man, emerging at last into the world of reality. And in that act an old soldier died, and a tramp was born: he would no longer ask for work, he would beg and be no longer ashamed of it.

Each visitor had a different story to tell: one elderly person, a native of Birmingham, delighted to sing the hymns he had learnt as a boy in the Salvation Army services. He assured me he said every night his *Pater noster,* possibly also learnt in Salvation Army classes. He carried his own tin, and just handed it in at the door to be filled with tea, adding that he took sugar. When the maid brought it out — we were sitting on a rustic form at the back — he took it, and at once proceeded to use his walking stick as a teaspoon, which seemed to me to do the job as effectively every bit as the latter. Amongst our callers were miners and steelworkers from South Wales and farm servants from East Anglia. There was one sad case which I remember very well; he was a man just past middle age, dressed quite decently, who once had been employed as a plumber by an urban council near Manchester. His trouble was, he said, that he could not sleep at night, for immediately he lay down, demons, spirits, imps and devils used him as a telephone exchange, to ring one another up and engage in conversation. Apart from this one delusion he was perfectly normal and discussed all other matters sanely and intelligently.

Two cases stand out in my memory and they both concern Welsh tramps, or I should really say two Welsh *men:* The first was a Cardi (a native of Cardiganshire); the second was a North Walian, making for Caergybi (Holyhead). I haven't much admiration for the Welshman as a tramp at all. A tramp is one who has contracted out of society, one who has no use for it, but since he has to live, he will, to that end, make use of it — he will beg from it and live on it, at the same time despising all its ways, values and aims. As such they approach our houses, and there is no pretence about it. One admires them for their honesty and their courage in making this final break. But the Welsh tramp does not approach our houses as a tramp at all, he comes as another Welshman, down on his luck at the moment it is true; and while his luck has abandoned him, he will not mind accepting a little help until times improve. He comes as another Welshman, almost as a neighbour, prepared to talk about the state of the churches, the value of the Sunday schools, as he could testify, if only in his own case. He will recall hearing some of the giants of the pulpit preach, indeed can give the text, and even give the sermon headings. The Welsh tramp has not broken with society at all, he is very much in it, and in his own sight still a part of it — the society, the Wales, in which the chapel, the Sunday school, the *seiat* and the *gymanfa ganu* play an important part, and he treasures his memory of them, for without them he would have no past at all.

To take the Cardi first, I must warn the reader that he will miss a great deal in this story unless he knows what one Cardiganshire man means to another. It is a relationship, leading to an appreciation of mutual traits, that cannot be paralleled in any human grouping known to history — close-knit, warm, loyal and lasting. My friend, for I must not call him a tramp, visited the vicarage when his round brought him into that part of the country — and believe me, he had a big round, for the sons of Cardiganshire are widely scattered. He did not call on small fry like curates, police constables and shop assistants; nothing less than incumbents, head-masters, sergeants, with a preference for Canons, Rural Deans, Archdeacons, superintendents of Police and Chief Constables. He brought gossip from one vicarage to another and from one police station to another, thus forming a very important link between one Cardi and another.

The other was a North Walian: he did not ask for anything, all he wanted to know was whether there was a Methodist chapel in the parish, whether it had a minister, and failing a minister — as was unfortunately for him the case at the time — could I tell him where one or two of the chief deacons lived. For the moment I thought he was one of the biggest rogues who had called on us: here was a man who would capitalise his early association with the denomination: remembering the close-knit fellowship of the chapel, the almost brotherly relationship that existed between one member and another, that no methodist would let another methodist down, nor would he be deaf to the plea of another now in distress, yes, remembering all this, he would exploit their friendliness and charity. But I changed my mind, the vision of a medieval pilgrim rose up before my eyes, a dutiful son of Mother Church travelling contentedly from one monastic house to another confident that he would find sympathy, kindness and charity in each one. Here was another, many centuries later, travelling in the same state of mind, happy, as a loyal son of Methodism, in the knowledge that he too would receive in every manse along the route — or, failing that, in some deacon's home — all the help and sympathy he needed to cheer him on his way. He had started from industrial South Wales and was already in mid-Wales, and seemed in very good fettle — a proof that he had not been disappointed so far. I have already said that he asked nothing of us at the vicarage: a son of methodism with so much faith and trust in its great heart and charity need not go outside it to ask for anything. I would advise all who may feel they would like to turn their backs on society and the rat race and embrace the life of a vagabond, to do so as a Cardi or as a Methodist!

My articles appeared mostly in the *Llan* and the *Western Mail,* during the time I was in Radnorshire, between 1926 and 1936, and show, if nothing else, that the life of a country priest can be as full as he cares to make it.

Towards the end of my stay in Radnorshire I started another kind of writing, more personal, limited to the perusal of my family only, especially my children. It all started because it was brought home to me that my children were growing up without knowing a word of Welsh. It was a matter in which we could do little and nobody was to blame: I had married an English girl which obviously meant that the language of the hearth was English. The children were ignorant, too, of the way of life of the rural community out in Welsh Wales in which I was brought up, so I started to write the story of my life for no other purpose at the time than the benefit and instruction of my children. They were after all half Welsh, and I felt it my duty as the representative and head of that half to see that they were properly informed of it, and that they fully and proudly accepted it. When I had really got a good start something like a fever — known I am sure to all writers — gripped me, and my pen could hardly keep pace with my memories as they crowded back on me. Chapters swelled out and had to be divided into two, new chapters suggested themselves to me once my memory began to open its gates, until, long before I finished it, I realised I had produced a book very much like the products of that very considerable school in England which write on the countryside, and not merely a simple story for children — rather it had grown to be a comprehensive picture of the many sides and aspects of the old Welsh rural society as it functioned when I was a boy.

TEN

Back to South Wales: Llanelly

IN THE AUTUMN OF 1935, the bishop, Dr John Morgan, asked me to go and see the vacant parish of Llanelly, Breconshire, lying between Brynmawr and Abergavenny. This meant no small excitement to a country family. We hired a taxi from the village to take us to see it, and I remember how charmed we were with that new country along the Usk, just as we entered it a mile or so before we came to Crickhowell. Then for another mile before we entered Gilwern great trees on each side of the road, partly tinted in their autumn gold, formed a canopy above the road and provided a long 'drive' as we entered the village. After the barrenness of the Radnor Forest, this country of trees and lush growth along the Usk simply captivated and enchanted us. We had lunch with the Rector and his wife and after that went to see the church and to take a look at the scattered parish from two or three vantage points. We liked the church and we liked the Rectory; indeed, we were delighted with the prospect of a change, and so enchanted with the beauty of this section of the Usk valley, that I failed to grasp that the hamlets and villages that were pointed out to me held in their location and distribution problems and difficulties that would continue with me for the next quarter of a century.

Of course we accepted it, and I wrote accordingly to the Bishop, but before we were due to move, a few cases of diphtheria broke out in the parish, amongst whom was my youngest daughter. It was a very light case but the doctor would not let us go until he had given the 'all clear'. I remember very well the exact time we arrived in our new parish, for the first service I attended at the church – as a private individual, for I had not been instituted, but I did read the lesson – was a memorial service for the late King George V. I had preached my last sermon at Llanfihangel Rhydithon at Evensong on Sunday 26 January 1936 from Phil. 4, *8 & 9*. I was conscious of what the occasion meant, and was deeply moved at the thought of parting with people that I had grown to like and to admire for the many qualities in their character. St Paul, in these verses, supplied me with just the thoughts and sentiments which I could so happily apply to the occasion. I preached it again a quarter of a century later when I parted from my people at Llanelly. As no artist and no poet destroy what they consider their best works, so did I not destroy this sermon, and as my relationship with the people of Llanelly had proved very similar to that which existed between me and my previous parishioners – and the thoughts and feelings that moved me were the same – I found as I re-read my old sermon that it said practically all I wanted to say.

The Rectory is one of the nicest I have ever seen, a three-storey house, built in 1913 – and by the way, everything that went to its building was brought by a canal which ran only a few yards away. The outbuildings consisted of saddle, or harness room, loose-box, stalls for two horses, a coach house, and running above them quite a spacious loft. As an indication of the change that had taken place since the outbuildings at Llanfihangel Rhydithon had been erected, there was no cowshed. Clergy, generally, had ceased to farm their own glebe, though I was told that nobody brought into Cardigan mart during the First World War a finer bunch of bullocks than the then Rector of Manordeify, the Rev. I. Harries Williams. As an indication of a greater change that had taken place since the Rectory at Gilwern was built, there were no horses, no harness, no coaches left to put in those roomy places built to accommodate them. The motor car had destroyed everything but itself.

There was a large orchard with very fine apple, plum, and damson trees, a good kitchen garden and a nice tennis lawn – everything affording a perfect paradise for the children, and a wonderful place to grow up in.

In the attic there were two bedrooms besides immense spaces that could also provide extra accommodation for beds, and all lined with high spacious cupboards, in which a dozen children could hide. In addition, the water-pipes ran along dark passages that could easily accommodate a similar number of children. Here, on wet days, the children, with their friends, played hide and seek, and as the cupboards held very large quantities of women's hats, furs and garments which had not been sold at the Jumble Sale, these provided ingenious minds with material to stage 'visits', 'funerals', plays and 'weddings', displaying fashions and costumes from the Crimean to the First World War. The children — and grandchildren — never cease to talk about the fun they had up in the attic and round the rectory generally.

Immediately I was settled in, the first thing I did was to take a good, long look at my new parish. I have said before that it was work I wanted, well, here at last it was. The population of the parish was 3,441, and was scattered in hamlets, villages, farms and cottages over its 4,000 acres. Its small acreage for a Welsh parish can be deceptive for it says nothing of its difficult terrain, rising sharply once it leaves the banks of the Usk to the grey uplands and the barren hill-country. One railway station in the parish was reputed to be the highest in Wales. The parish church was up on the hillside, a mile each from Clydach and Gilwern, the two main villages, and was surrounded not by houses but by one of the finest circle of yews that I have ever seen, altogether thirteen of them; once they numbered sixteen, but three of those facing north have perished. The simple fact that they were old was sufficient to make them at once the objects of my interest and care; evidence of that may be seen in the form of a stout chain with which I tied together the two halves of one of them, which were in danger of splitting and parting. Their greatest enemy is the calm fall of heavy snow, which, as they are many-branched and long-branched, can weigh hundred-weights and bring down quite sturdy branches. When it blows hard they escape this danger. It is said they are as old as the church; they are old enough, according to tradition, to have supplied the bowmen of Gwent with wood for their long bows. I tried more than once to replace the three missing on the north side, but as soon as they reached the size of a Christmas tree, somebody came along and cut them down, possibly for a few pints.

Besides the parish church, there were three mission churches and down in Gilwern a building which we called the Church Room where the Sunday school, the mid-week communions and the Lenten services were held. It had a movable altar which was put on one side when parochial meetings, jumble sales, concerts and plays were held. The mission churches, too, were all-purpose buildings with provision for shutting off the sanctuary when they were put to secular use. One of the most serious drawbacks of the parish was — and is — that it has no recognised, acknowledged centre. It is only clergy who have had experience of such a parish who know how difficult, indeed how impossible it is, to organise any meeting or function that will secure the consent and the support of the whole parish. It divides itself into four areas to which the people were conscious they belonged, each with its own mission church, leaving the parish church, along with the Church Room in Gilwern, to supply the spiritual needs of the village and the largely agricultural area around. In each of these mission churches, there was a Sunday school and I, as if I had already far too little to do, had to start another — at the parish church — so that we had five Sunday schools. In starting the latter, I had more serious motives than creating records, but looking back upon that period, I suppose it was really a record, for could there be at that time another Anglican parish with five Sunday schools! They were not big Sunday schools but they needed frequent visiting and encouraging. When I got a car, I could visit two on a Sunday afternoon and was thus able to keep in constant touch with them. When Christmas came it meant five Sunday school parties. In the autumn we had four harvest festivals which meant five special harvest festival preachers, for the parish church demanded two, one on a weekday as well as on Sunday. The problem for me was that I was exhausting the sources of special preachers in a wide countryside, until I began to be reminded: 'I was only there three or four years ago'. Counting in addition the festivals in which I was myself the special preacher, I must have sung:

'We plough the fields and scatter . . .' at least a dozen times every year.

Visiting was made difficult because of bad roads and the hilly nature of the terrain, but I had a curate. However, in a short time after my arrival I received a letter from the bishop saying he was taking him away because he had discovered in talks with my predecessor that the parish could not possibly pay his stipend. This was a great disappointment and a blow, for I had already intended to make a forward drive, but the bishop was proved to be right; the finances of the church were, indeed, in a parlous state — and what wonder, they were the years of depression which had made notorious the town of Brynmawr and district. Curates had to be paid and even when paid in full their salary was in all conscience low enough. The bishop only did his duty by these young men. He was taken away from what at that time must have been the poorest parish in the diocese and given to one of the wealthiest parishes in Swansea. But then he was sure of his stipend. At that time curates went to parishes which could pay for them and not to the parishes that needed them.

It was a good thing my plans were only in the paper stage for this new turn of events compelled me to overhaul the whole of my thinking. It became plain that I could do no more than just carry on — a sufficient feat in itself. Plenty of work is good for one, it can even be exhilarating, but what I was faced with was not so much work as a host of difficulties. Nor was I unaware that one of my predecessors had broken down, so much to the distress of Bishop Bevan that he vowed he would never again allow the Rector of Llanelly to be without a colleague. But Bishop Morgan, new to the diocese, did not know this. I doubt, however, that if he did know, he would have acted differently —at that time — for he was not a man who did things without weighing very carefully the pros and cons of the matter. Its immediate effect was to remove one of my difficulties, namely, the financial; now, with a little care the money might stretch to meet the ordinary needs of the parish. Perhaps I was all the happier for it, for I have never been a good hand at begging, or collecting, money; indeed, I have always hated it; nevertheless, I am a tremendous admirer of those priests who have the gift to

invent ways and organize means of getting it in, for it has
been so necessary to do so in recent years.

My bishop did not forget me; in twelve months, with more
generous grants, I was able to get a curate again, and so it
continued till well after the Second World War when the
shortage, not of money this time, but of men, deprived me
once more of a colleague.

Readers may wonder how, with all these mission
churches, I was able to provide Sunday services for them all.
But then I had three faithful Lay-readers. I owe more to
Lay-readers, I think, than any other priest in the present
century, and I would like here to pay tribute to their loyal
and faithful service, rendered gladly, freely, without any
thought of pay or even expenses. One of them worked long
hours every day in the pit, but he was ready again on Sunday
to take the morning service at his mission church, Sunday
school in the afternoon and then in the evening take a service
in one of the other mission churches. Fred was a working
miner and he spoke like a working man. He was no scholar,
but he knew his Bible, he knew life, and a hard life, he knew
also the way the minds of the working men worked, he knew
their temptations and weaknesses. Such a man was invaluable
to the church. What other knowledge or fitness did a man
need to preach the gospel to his fellow men? At first, before I
began to work all this out and to see it all in this light, I had
my misgivings, for his speech, though ample and ready
enough, was broad like that of his mates, and lacked the
refinement, the polish and the correctness that comes from
acquaintance with books, especially grammar books! I heard
him read the lessons once, and he said 'suppley-ker', and I
thought that such mis-pronunciations in the reading of the
lessons, and such homely phrases in the pulpit, must surely
jar on the ears of the people. But it didn't, for he spoke
exactly as they spoke, for I daresay they all pronounced
sepulchre as 'suppley-ker'. It was my pronunciation and my
language that must have appeared odd and strange to them,
and also, in places, meaningless, for those who had reached
middle-age were the first generation to use the English
language after the general decay of the Welsh; and their grasp
and use of it was not extensive.

While on this point I may as well refer to another matter
which bears a close resemblance to it: One Sunday evening in
my curate days I had to go and preach at the parish church
whose service must have started half an hour earlier than ours
at the mission church, for I was back at the church door as
the congregation was coming out — the service having been
taken by a young man who was under instruction with a view to
becoming a Lay-reader. As the congregation filed past me on
the way out I caught words of praise for the sermon, even of
wonder, for he was only a working lad. Later on in the
evening I met one of the church officials and asked him
about the sermon. It was evident that he too had been greatly
impressed, but what really moved them was the brief
peroration at the end, winding up with Cardinal Wolsey's
words in Shakespeare's *Henry VIII*. It was my turn to be
surprised now, that so trite, so well-known, so hackneyed a
quotation from Shakespeare should move or impress anybody. I, personally, would be ashamed to quote those words,
deeming them so pedestrian as to fall to the level of a cliché.
My quotation would have to be far less familiar, even obscure,
but one which would show a wider knowledge and a deeper
appreciation of the Bard. I tried to imagine the reaction of a
really profound Shakespearean scholar at such a hackneyed,
over-used quotation. But then, to a lover of Shakespeare he
could not be quoted too often, and as for my less familiar
and more obscure passages, they would be as well known and
as familiar to him as Wolsey's words to me. So the
Shakespearean scholar can be ruled out, indeed, on the other
hand, he can be roped in as an ally and an admirer. This
taught me a valuable lesson, and I have thought a great deal
about it since, and indeed despised myself for being what I
then must have been — a snob. This quotation from
Shakespeare that Sunday evening must have been new to half
the congregation, and to the other half fresh, with a nostalgic
tinge and appeal about it for having lain in oblivion since
school days. Clergy go into retreat into semi-monastic
Anglican institutions; it would benefit some of us a great deal
more if we went for a week to work underground, in a steel
works, or in a factory to discover for ourselves the general
reach of the ordinary man's thinking, his level of convers-

ation and his interests in general.

I am not going to fill my pages with details of parish work, rather do I want to mention things of interest that I came across, or met with, in the course of my work as a parish priest. In addition to my three Lay-readers I had now a curate and the work was gathering momentum. I was on the point of bringing out earlier blue-prints when the war broke out and everything was put back in cold storage again.

I joined the Home Guard, being the first at the local Police Station to enrol. Our commanding officer was the local school master, who had a fund of dry humour. I could fill a book on the funny things that happened during the earlier months of our training — believe me, *Dad's Army* is not far from the actual truth of things. One of my worries was how to cover all our church windows, for they were all, as well as the Rectory, in quite prominent positions; it was made all the more difficult because of the officiousness of the half-trained special police, conscious only of the new power they had acquired in the community. I think that all of us who joined the voluntary bodies that sprang up at the commencement of the war, were apt to be too conscious of the powers we presumed they conferred upon us, and like all untrained, or partly-trained, troops, went about our duties in a brusque, officious manner — and no nonsense about it. We stopped cars and asked questions and no doubt caused a lot of unnecessary annoyance, but in time we matured, and went about our duties as volunteer citizens rather than as billeted or garrison troops — a comparison that would not be very much overdrawn of a few aggressive citizens when they first put uniform on.

Rationing came and we had to abandon our prejudice against margarine, mixing it with the small quantity of butter allowed, and never again to return exclusively to butter, as we were told that margarine was more nutritious, and that it was not as likely to lead to heart trouble. We suffered the same inconveniences as most country parishes, and they are all too well remembered to be recorded here, except to say that since our churches were so isolated, we may have suffered more in the matter of attendances. My curate left me to join up as a chaplain but I was able to get another without much delay. I was fortunate in all my young colleagues and was happy with them.

Later on, and for the last twelve years of my ministry when I was getting older and the spring had departed from my legs, I had to toil on alone, partly because curates were getting scarcer, but principally because my bishop had come to the conclusion that the parish was not a suitable one for the training of a curate, as he had to live in another part of the parish where personal supervision of, and guidance in, his work and life could not be given. I did not quarrel with the Bishop's decision, though I had always considered it as one of my first duties and obligations to my curates to see that they were properly trained in all that appertained to their personal life, in general pastoral work, and in giving them an example of hard, dogged work, and I must say they responded with a right goodwill.

As ours was the only burial ground in use in the parish it followed that all burials took place there. That meant that funerals took up many of my afternoons — and the whole afternoon, for, as I have stated, the parish church stood a good mile up the hill. In addition, it was the custom, universal throughout Wales, to hold a short service of reading and prayer in the house before taking the body out, round which the neighbours gathered to sing a hymn before the procession moved off. All this was called 'the rising of the funeral'. As I was for some time the only ordained minister in the parish, though it possessed eleven chapels, it meant that I was asked in numerous cases to go and 'rise' many funerals in nonconformist homes. It was not without its reward for once you had shared their sorrow and endeavoured to lighten it with readings and prayers you were for ever afterwards held in a new light and were secure in their esteem and affection. In this way did I get to know intimately many of my parishioners.

Our main churchyard — we had another two, but full these many years — was above the church, a bleak, open place, facing east. Here I experienced some of the wettest, coldest, squalliest afternoons of my life, but it was not allowed to interfere with the full service; there was no dropping of even the last hymn round the grave. No concession whatsoever was

made to the weather or to shivering, dripping bodies – this
would be dishonouring the dead. Fortunately for me, having
taken so many funerals, I knew the service by heart for no
book could be held open, nor could any umbrella withstand
the fury of the squalls. Men, women and children attended
the funerals, a fact that might make strangers conclude that
the Welsh liked funerals. Behind it all is another explanation.
Funerals are always large where the community feeling is
strong and this was especially so in the mining district in the
upper half of the parish. The *Hebrwng* – a word used in
Wales for that last, friendly act of the host and hostess in
accompanying their visitors a part of their way home – is
often used also for a funeral, the *sending* (in its Anglicised
form) of the departed a part of his way home – at least as far
as the grave. In medieval times when the sense of community
was stronger, large funerals must have been the normal thing
for the Prayer Book envisages the presence of a large number
of the parishioners. Private funerals, as well as private
baptisms and weddings, are completely contrary to the mind
of the church as expressed in these services.

As I have always been particularly careful that everything
that is done in church should be done correctly, seemly and
reverently, I always, in leading the procession from the
church to the grave, proceeded unhurriedly and in silence, as
befits the occasion, for one can never feel dignified or
reverent in rushing, chasing or running. I had no difficulty at
all in maintaining the due standard of dignity and solemnity,
until I engaged a new grave-digger, the nicest, friendliest man
in the parish, but a man utterly devoid of any sense of the
fitness of things. He would join me at the church door and
would walk at my side all the way to the grave which could,
depending upon the site of the grave, be a full two hundred
yards away, and which would take a considerable time as the
bearers had to take two or three rests, especially when the
ground was soft and slipping feet made as much progress
backwards as forwards. There was nothing wrong in my
grave-digger walking by my side, though the previous one
always walked in front of me, but Bob starting at the church
door would regale me with a summary of the main events, or
of the main qualities, in the life of the deceased: 'He were a

rare lad he were, I mind him and me going to Abergavenny Fair and as we had run through our money he says to me "Bob, let's go to the boxing booth". He was good with his fists he was, an' he had a fight and won, so with ten bob we started enjoying the fair again'.

On another occasion it might be a woman. 'Aye, she were a tartar, she went through three husbands and she would have gone through a fourth if she could 'ave had one. She were that strong and wide she could knock a man down as easy as knocking a chair over. Aye, I mind one night at the Red Cow . . .' While I was committing her to the ground, being only human, I am not sure that moving round this conscious act, in the margin of my mind, there was not a figure 'strong and wide', scattering men and chairs in all directions. Some may ask why I didn't shut him up, but no Christian would have the heart to tell that kind, friendly, open face to shut up. And, again, what was wrong with it, all the parish knew her and why should not the parson know her too. Can clergy in the country become too squeamish, and insist on standards and observances in which the countryman can see no point at all? The reader will see that underneath the priest and very near the surface there still lurks the countryman.

While we are on the subject of funerals, I might as well say here all I have to say about them. Having 'risen' so many nonconformist funerals in addition to my own, I had quite mastered the art of extempore prayer. Nonconformists to this day do not think much of a minister who cannot address his creator face to face and not through the medium of a book, though they have now printed forms of prayers and printed forms of the burial service. Still the fact that I could 'rise' a funeral without having to have recourse to a book commended me greatly to nonconformist families. With regard to our own service I knew it off by heart so that it must have appeared extempore to the congregation.

The Book of Common Prayer, excellent as it is, failed the priest, and the occasion, sometimes. For example, all too often I buried a miner killed underground, but there was no prayer in it to suit such a sad and tragic occasion and one felt one could not bury him as one did — and as is generally envisaged in the Prayer Book — an old man gathered in in his season like a shock of corn.

Another occasion — out of many — when the Prayer Book had nothing to say was the celebration of St David's day. If a priest wished to remember on this important day, national institutions and movements, our schools and colleges, our agriculture and industries and our leaders in church and state, he had to fall back on himself. Where parish priests have led for many years, the church, moving all too slowly, comes along in time and sets the seal of approval on the practice, as has been done in recent revisions, in allowing, for example, extempore prayer in certain parts of the services.

As the parish church was an old one and a very prominent landmark, it attracted a large number of visitors, and one was quite accustomed to see strangers, and sometimes members of other churches within the parish amongst the congregation. It was not unknown for some of the latter to become enamoured of our manner of worshipping and to seek membership. I need not here say that I never during my long ministry, tried to influence any member of another Christian body to join us, nor did I know of any of my brethren who stooped to such a low practice. The days of proselytising were over. Nor did I see it amongst other Christian bodies in the parish. Most of the chapels were rather exclusive in their membership: certain of the families, in a settled community such as ours, had long acquired the leadership and were not anxious to see an influx of strangers who might upset the balance and dispute a leadership that had proved successful along the years. What could happen sometimes — and did happen — was that one of our members might be invited by a friend or a neighbour to come to their chapel: 'Oh, Mrs Jones, we've got a wonderful preacher at our chapel next Sunday evening, and you must come and hear him, he's the Rev. Morgan Morgans, he's a B.A., a B.D. and a Ph.D.' — and of course we would miss Mrs Jones that Sunday evening.

After the war, the Heads of the Valleys road was built right up through the centre of the parish. It made a considerable change in the village of Blackrock, sweeping away a number of houses including our mission church. Originally it was a Primitive Methodist chapel which was bought by one of my predecessors. It had also a small burial ground from which the bodies were transferred down to the parish church. I was quite impressed by the obvious concern of the authorities and of the men who carried out this very unpleasant job, that it should be done reverently and expeditiously. Care was taken that the gravestones should go with them and continue their vigil over the same body.

Here, perhaps, is the best place to mention the fact that things belonging to the church can so easily get lost. For example, one of these gravestones, if folks had not kept a strict watch, could very well have been lost, for they are useful for many purposes. Gravestones have found their way into private houses before — at one time there was a popular cheese sold in Carmarthenshire called *Resurrection cheese* from the fact that it was pressed on a gravestone bearing that word amongst others. There was a house in my parish, where once lived the churchwarden and where a stone bench for the salting of pig carcasses had been built of two or three gravestones. These flitches could contain all sorts of startling and shocking sentences — even such a one as 'Died 1798'. The action of some of the clergy, and of the churchwardens — often annually changed — of taking to their homes church documents, registers and other things was a practice fraught with great dangers. With the death of the wardens or of the incumbents, these were often lost, or they found their way to unauthorised persons. Llanelly parish, through some neglect or other, had lost a farm given to it for the benefit of the poor. I was just in time at a sale at Llanbadarn Fawr Rectory, Radnorshire, to save the church safe containing all the registers. It should be made obligatory on all clergy and church officers to notify the bishop when they take anything away from the church, even for the purpose of protecting it, and to receive his permission.

It was not our intention to build another mission church at Blackrock, as I had now organised a Sunday bus service to gather in all our people for a united evening service at the parish church. I had only therefore to provide a monthly celebration which I did in one of the homes of our members. One person in particular on whom I depended so much for help in running the mission, the Sunday school and the weekly meetings was re-housed in a part of the parish too hilly and awkward for the bus to negotiate. I was particularly pleased at the prospect of now having her help in this isolated and outlandish mission, so difficult for us to reach and supervise, but to my great disappointment she never settled down there at all, and the parish can be said to have lost a church family.

Since the building of so many housing estates in all parts of the country and the breaking up of settled neighbourhoods in our large towns, and the herding of families amongst complete strangers, we have learnt — and for the first time — how strong the ties, family, social, religious and neighbourly, are that form a community, and the havoc, social and psychological, that follows when it is broken up. I remember an old fellow-curate of mine who became Vicar of a big housing estate round Manchester saying that church people, even people who had been churchwardens in their old parishes, felt no interest in their new church, and never came near. The practice of religion is by its very nature a community activity, and before the church can make much headway in these new concentrations of population, it will have first to build up a sense of community.

Having lost a curate owing to the unsatisfactory state of the finances, I decided to remedy things by introducing the Sunday envelope system, but it was not viewed at all favourably except by the church officers who had of course to pay the bills. It took quite a bit of explaining and two or three sermons. With a few I only succeeded by assuring them that they would be anonymous and that the numbers would be known only to the Rector. In time it became generally accepted, and proved to be the backbone of our finances. Upon what principle people gave previously, and indeed in some cases after the envelopes were introduced, must remain a mystery. In commending some sort of sacrifice in giving, I went a step further and stretched my Lenten self-denial to cover even Easter Sunday, reminding my people, as the festival came round, of my self-abnegation, in the hope that it might move a few to act in sympathy. But whether anyone ever did must remain another mystery. I must make one thing quite plain here, I am not suggesting or hinting that anyone else should follow my example. Normally I would gladly have accepted an Easter offering for I could do with it — it is the ancient customary right of every parish priest, and as a rule churches value this one opportunity of the year to show their gratitude to him, and their appreciation of what he is trying to do amongst them, which, in turn, gladdens the heart of the recipient, and braces him to strive all the more in his work, to preserve that appreciation and goodwill.

Nobody for one moment would regard the calling of a parish priest as one that could endanger life, or present hazards such as daily face miners and workers in other industries. But one day I thought my last moment had come when I was confronted by an irate farmer on the yard. He was filling manure into a cart, and immediately he saw me he rushed at me waving a dirty, four-pronged muck fork about my head, and charging me with trying to establish a right of way along the way I had come. As a son of the farm, I had always, if it was possible, cut across fields and over hedges, to shorten the distance in visiting and also to save time. After a lot of explanation, and assuring him that I had no intention of doing anything of the kind, he cooled down. It seems he had had trouble with neighbours who were claiming a right of way somewhere along the path I had taken. As I thought of the incident afterwards I could understand his fear and his outburst, for after all the Rector of the Parish is not an ordinary parishioner. What if one of those who claimed a right of way had seen me coming that way? He could make good use of it by protesting that surely the Rector knows all about rights of way, for he has in his possession the old tithe maps and other ancient documents and terriers — he ought to know. So a parish priest has to be doubly careful even when he is only ambling leisurely through the woods.

Though few clergy, if any, die from muck-fork attacks, the profession is not without its casualties, generally in the form of breakdowns. The clerical profession does impose a restraint upon its members, and it does involve a degree of withdrawal from the social and secular life of the age, yet there are in all parishes those homes — or havens — where, in the company of intimate friends, who understand he too, is human, the priest can relax and indulge in the lighter moods of life. Nevertheless, on most occasions and in most places he can never forget that he is a man in holy orders, and it may be that a number of the casualties are attributable in some degree to this restraint and repression, whereas in another profession they might have come through unscathed.

When I went to Radnorshire first and was met with 'Yes Surr' 'No Surr' from the farm servants and from a large number of the parishioners, I concluded that it was a sign and a proof of the native refinement of the people, but after a time I began to suspect that I had misconstrued their attitude towards me: It was not so much that they were trying to show respect to me, as to say: 'keep your distance, you are not one of us; don't come too near, keep to your own world'. The 'Surr' was to keep me from coming too far and too intimately into their own world.

As one who likes all survivals from an older world I was quite charmed by the habit of some of the older women of curtsying to me, until I began to suspect this too, as I had come to suspect the 'surring'. Anyhow, at first I was quite charmed with it for it was a new experience to me, for we Welsh-speaking folk curtsied to nobody and 'surred' nobody. In their earlier years these old women had been in service in gentlemen's houses and as they ranked me with them, I was given the same treatment. I could have been forgiven if I had thought at first that it indicated a sort of servility, a survival from the time when the gap between the serf and his master was real and wide. Nothing of the kind; it was, I believe, defensive behaviour, in case I came too near to them — unless they were ill, when of course they would accept the comforts of my spiritual care. Servility indeed! Nothing of the kind, these old ladies were very forthright and were not beyond telling me if they disagreed with the way I was running things. It was with the most graceful and courtly curtsy, I was once told: 'I am not coming to church again!'

During the war a large number of our own and American soldiers were stationed in the parish and in the immediate neighbourhood. In our parish, too, was built a large American hospital, so that on the whole we saw a very large number of troops of all types. We became familiar with clashes between white and black American soldiers, and we were subjected to some caustic remarks for allowing our girls to dance with blacks. The senior American chaplain at the hospital was a Roman Catholic, but saw to it that the protestants had all their rights and privileges, and I suppose that it was as one of the protestants I was called in sometimes to assist. Pay was quite generous, but spasmodic, generally in the form of large cartons of American cigarettes.

When the soldiers began to arrive in considerable numbers, we opened our church room to them twice a week, so that they might have somewhere to go, and to give our young people the opportunity to meet them and entertain them. My wife supervised the ladies of the church who helped with the refreshments. Here, I spent most of my Tuesday and Friday evenings, often standing at the door to take the small nominal charge, but when I got a substitute I just mingled amongst the young men. Even so, I remained a mystery to many American soldiers until they left us: some called me *Father,* some, mostly the coloured men, the *Preacher-man,* some *Padre* or *Minister* and some even *Rabbi*! One evening I had noticed two American soldiers arguing and looking at me; presently one of them got up and dragged his friend with him, ostensibly to have it out with me and to find out what I really was. His question was: 'Do you in your church read the Bible or sing the Bible?' I said: 'We sing the Bible'. And he turned to his friend and said, poking him hard in the chest as he did so, 'Didn't I tell you!' as if at last the whole matter was clear to him. I gave that answer because I thought it possible that he might have strayed in on one occasion to an Anglican church and had heard them chanting the psalms.

A lot of the American soldiers had been drinking before they turned in and pushed past me at the door without taking the least notice of me or my little phrase that we made a small charge just to cover the light and the heat; then another American who had been a witness to all this would come up to me and say: 'Don't take too much notice of them; here's a pound to cover their admission'. One met with such a mixture of crudeness and refinement, ignorance and gentleness. What amazed me was the large number of American soldiers, who never drank or smoked. At this early age they were inveterate souvenir hunters: at one of the dances a young soldier accidentally dropped his saucer and it broke into dozen pieces. He offered profuse apologies and wanted to pay. We of course would have nothing of the kind and told him not to worry about it. As all our crockery was stamped with the name of the parish, LLANELLY CHURCH ROOM, he asked if he might keep that section. It is probably today decorating a mantelpiece in some part of America to remind one lad of his stay in a parish with two unpronounceable letters or sounds in it.

During the war, too, a large number of evacuees arrived in the parish — the first coach-load or two from London. I went down to the village to meet them: No family or individual had been allocated by name to any home, and it was curious to notice how rushes were made for the cleanest looking. At the end one gipsy family was left to be taken along elsewhere. There were none for us this first evening; however, a short time later a mother with her small boy came along. After a time they left, for the mother had found a home where the boy could be cared for and she could go out to work. We next had a father and mother, and a daughter of about fourteen, who attended the County School at Brynmawr. This girl was utterly selfish and spoiled. She gave way to exhibitions of temper and really frightened her mother whom she would sometimes lock up in her room for an hour, or lock herself up and scream the place down. More than once things got so bad that we had to 'phone the father to come home. After a year or so they got a house of their own and left.

Next, there came to us a Miss Morgan with her housekeeper, Mrs Okay. Miss Morgan before the war had kept a private school for girls at Brighton. Originally they were three, but Miss Robinson had died since they had arrived in the parish. The two lived with us until they died. The three are buried in the parish church-yard, but no monument marks the spot. It was rather sad, for they were such nice, refined ladies, and Miss Morgan in addition posessed a very strong sense of humour. It was a pity they ever left Brighton and their friends.

Another type of evacuee now arrived in the parish — an Approved School — and was accommodated at one of the mansions in the parish, Ty Mawr, once the residence of a branch of the Crawshay family. Though I rather liked the new experience, this again added to my work, for I used to make frequent visits to the school and once a week went down to take the morning service. They attended the parish church on Sunday mornings and completely filled the North aisle. Some of them had quite good voices and three or four of them were always in the choir. They behaved well, even better than our own choristers, due undoubtedly to the fact that they were accustomed to discipline.

All this brought more work to the parish priest, but I was strong and healthy. The reader will remember that earlier on I said there was considerable discontent amongst the curates at the prospect of being 'buried alive' in the country, with little or nothing to do, and that it was work we required. Well, in my case at any rate work had at last come, more than making up for the comparative ease of the nine years spent in Radnorshire.

ELEVEN

Eighteenth-Century Predecessor: Letters and Legends

IT WILL BE REMEMBERED that before I came away from Radnorshire I had started writing the story of my upbringing for my children. When I came to my new parish I had of course to put it on one side, but I never forgot it and in the dark evenings I often took it out of the drawer, and when the weather was such that one could do no visiting I worked away at it so that at the end of the war I had finished it. The question now was: 'Where do we go from here?' Realising that I had produced something more ambitious and embracing than a mere story for my children, I had visions of having it published. When this became a definite aim, I read books and magazines on how to prepare the manuscript and how to approach publishers — and what publishers. Just at this time I read A.L. Rowse's *A Cornish Childhood* and as this invited comparisons, I became all the more convinced that my manuscript stood a good chance. I was fortunate, too, in that there lived in the parish three persons who had written books — all with doctorates — and so up to Pantybeibau, to Dr Noelle Davies went my manuscript. When I saw her next she was most enthusiastic and said: 'Oh, Rector you must have this published' — but how, where? The question again was: 'Where do we go from here?' I decided to go into Abergavenny library, for I knew there was there quite a sizeable panel of books on the countryside. These I took all down and noted the publishers, and I discovered that most of them had been published by Batsford. To Batsford, therefore, it went, set out and packed according to the best advice of my many *Helps to Authors*. I was prepared now to wait for three months, for these 'Helps' assured us writers that publishing firms were stacked to the ceiling with manuscripts. It was, however, suggested that at the end of that time a postcard might be sent to them reminding them that somewhere between floor and ceiling a very precious manuscript lay. I had not to wait those three months, not even three weeks, for in a fortnight Harry Batsford wrote to me to say that they were happy to accept my manuscript, and offering me terms that were, indeed, generous. This good news just shot me up to the sky and I walked on the clouds for the next few weeks. Towards the end of the year it was published under the title: *Welsh Country Upbringing* and in a short time became a 'best seller'. Only those who have had a book published know what a thrill it is to stand outside a bookshop and see in the window your own book, bearing your own name! My cup was full, but more was poured into it in the shape of letters of appreciation that came from far and wide, assuring me of the pleasure people had derived from reading it. But what I like to remember above all the others is what I was told by a neighbouring priest, who said his father who had had a similar upbringing to mine, had read it three or four times in the last year of his life. He had now reached a great age and his memory was impaired, so, when he finished reading it, he picked it up again after a few days and read it over once more, forgetting that he had read it before, each time finding it fresh and absorbing. I like to recall this story and I am glad that I gave so much pleasure to an old man who, in the book, found his youth once again, and died a young man, revelling in the health and strength of those early years.

I do not want to mention visiting again only to say that I and my colleague kept at it; and whereas I could make fifty or sixty in Stockport, in Llanelly we had to cut it down to twenty-five a week. Even at that figure it demanded, owing to the nature of the terrain, far greater physical exertion than double that number in a town. From all I can gather, visiting is not given the priority in church work that it was given in my curate days. One must expect changes, many changes — and big changes — to take place in fifty or sixty years, especially in view of the rapid progress in scientific knowledge and technological advances. The general practitioner does not visit his patients now as he used to; if they possibly can they are expected to come to the surgery, that is, to visit *him*. Cases that he would at one time treat at home, are now sent to hospital. It would be naïve to expect that parishes should — or even could — be worked today exactly in the same way as they were fifty or sixty years ago, but that visiting should be the first casualty still puzzles me.

It was only by visiting my people that I got to know them so well, nor was my visiting confined to church families; for example, if a church family lived in the farthest house of a row of houses (called ranks locally) one could not pass without noticing other folks in the row, many of whom after the manner of working people would very likely be sitting on a chair by the door. Often I was told of somebody who was ill in the area and was asked if I would go and visit him or her. I could not refuse such a request, and I never did, for though there were four chapels in that part of the parish, there was no resident minister. In my twenty-six years as Rector of the parish I found enough evidence to convince me that though these families, of their own choice, had abandoned the church and followed their preference to worship elsewhere and in another way, there still lingered a belief amongst them that, as Rector of the parish, they had a claim to my services. They did not air it openly nor did they even hint that that was so, still, I could not be unaware of it.

Strange and proud convictions are sometimes entertained by quite poor and obscure people that they are people of aristocratic birth, only that they have been robbed of their birthright. An old spinster lady, living on her own, told me she had a far better claim than Sir J. Ll. to the estate and mansion of Pen . . . Indeed, as I looked at her tall figure and noted her refined features, I felt that, dressed up in the costumes and frills of the Victorian age, she would quite look the part of the dowager lady of the house.

After the war there was considerable excitement in many families in the valleys of north Monmouthshire, and in the top end of my parish, for efforts were being made to lay claim to a vast fortune of many hundreds of millions of pounds that had accumulated from property, mostly in land, left by a family that had emigrated from Llanelly parish. On this land in later years was built the greater part of New York City and the value of the estate by now was considered to be incalculable. A lot of the work devolved on me for I was asked to trace relatives and establish links through means of the registers. After three or four years it all died down as suddenly as it had arisen, and all the dreams vanished. I shall not be surprised if in ten or fifteen years it is all resurrected once again, for working people love excitements of this kind.

There were in the parish amongst the working people descendants of old Norman families settled in Breconshire, notably the Gunters and the Walbeoffs, the latter name in many cases having been shortened to Walby, for which I severely rebuked some of the families. Thoughts of a distinguished lineage meant nothing to them today. They were, as miners, far more interested in a rise of a few shillings in their weekly wage.

While visiting one day in a hamlet at the top end of the parish, I came across a very peculiar idea concerning motherhood — or rather pregnancy: I was asked, 'Rector, do you think that woman should come out to church in that condition?' 'Why,' I said, 'what condition?' 'Well,' she continued 'you know she's expecting — I never went out of the house for the last three months before my babies were born, but she's that bold and brazen!' I said I could see nothing wrong at all in it, it was motherhood and so God had ordained it. I didn't say any more at the moment, but if I did, I am sure I would have said that if there was anything to be ashamed about it, let the men share in that shame, and if there is to be any going into hiding, let the men go as well, for anything short of that would appear to me unfair, as they are so evidently accomplices in the act — or in the crime — depending upon the way it is looked at.

Sex was not to be talked about amongst these people, it was not even to be thought about and when somebody moved about freely exhibiting obvious signs that sex had been at work, even that had to be suppressed. Women hid the fact as long as they could, but in time I could detect it as quick as any mother, for if one saw a woman out on a warm sunny day, wearing a loose mackintosh, it was a sure sign. I talked the matter over with my wife for I felt sure that she, through the Mothers' Union could do something about it, and I would take advantage of certain festivals in the Church's Calendar to talk about the joy and the sanctity of motherhood, especially those in which we honoured the Blessed Virgin Mary whose example has bestowed dignity and sanctity upon motherhood for all time.

When I first heard of this taboo I reacted towards it as any Christian would, as something outrageous and as casting gross infamy upon motherhood. But I had the habit too of thinking over things that I had seen or heard during the day, and this occupied a good many hours of my thinking during the next few days. And as other beliefs and superstitions concerning motherhood came back to me, it occurred to me that this taboo could have a very different explanation: it was widely held at one time that if a pregnant mother, when she was out, was frightened by a snake or a rat or some similar creature, the mark of that animal which frightened her would be produced on the body of her child, where, in her fright, she happened to put her hands. Mothers therefore steeled themselves against falling victims to the first instinctive impulse to lift the hands to the face and so shut out the sight of the object which caused the fright. As I thought about it, I wondered whether this had anything to do with it, and that mothers, especially in the last three months or so, would keep indoors so as not to lay themselves open to these dangers. Readers of Mary Webb's *Precious Bane* will remember that poor Prue was, as she said, 'hare-shotten', because when her mother was out one day a hare crossed the path she was taking.

In 1957 I was made Rural Dean of Crickhowell, an appointment that gave me very great pleasure though it added to my work; but I was healthy and strong, and now possessed a car. From time to time I was called upon to visit churches and vicarages; in the case of the latter to help speed up attention to complaints. I know that in one department I took my work very seriously, and that was in the inspection of the registers. I cannot say that I found any sign of indifference as to their state, or any neglect of safety precautions. The greatest actual enemy of all records in churches, and of all books for that matter, is damp. Having old registers of my own, I got into touch with the National Library of Wales with the result that four or five were sent up for repair and re-binding — and a most excellent work was done on them and at a very low cost. These I used to take round with me to show what could be done with those that were beginning to fray and to come apart. Nevertheless, I think that in all theological colleges, talks should be given in the last year on the irreplaceable value of these local records. Possibly a member of the staff of the National Library could be invited to give a lecture on their value and on the help the Library can give in the shape of repairs, etc, and generally to emphasise the responsibility that lies on the shoulders of all who have in their care ancient documents. It could be extended to give an illustration of how history has been corrected when a research student decided that, instead of copying blindly from previous writers, he would look up entries in the parish register, only to find that since the object of the research was born on such and such a date, or that he died on such and such a date, he could not possibly have been present at such a place, and therefore not responsible for what was generally attributed to him.

Llanelly parish until the advent of the Rev. Arthur Griffiths in 1850 had been worked as a chapel-of-ease under Llangattock, and served by a curate, one of whom in the early years of the last century had been Carnhuanawc (1787-1848). Earlier, it had been served by the Rev. Henry Thomas Payne (1759-1832) who, graduating from Balliol in 1780, and ordained in 1783, came direct to Llanelly as his first curacy, being supervised and helped undoubtedly by his father who was the incumbent of the neighbouring parish. Henry Thomas Payne was a distinguished and patriotic son of Wales, keenly interested in the Eisteddfod and a careful observer of Welsh life and custom in his native Breconshire. Later in life he became Archdeacon of Carmarthen. Incredible as it may seem, this young man, two years after ordination, was signing himself (1785) 'Rural Dean of the Third Part of Brecon'. He must have been appointed over the heads of all the senior clergy, including his father! We must be grateful that his Bishop had the courage and the discernment to appoint him for he proved himself to be a most conscientious Rural Dean, untiring in the pursuit of his duties, fearless and outspoken in his reports — even noting sad deficiences in the general state of things in his father's church at Llangattock where he found that the edifice had been allowed to get into a 'very delapidated and indeed dangerous state, the communion table . . . but an indifferent one', the linen 'much stained. There are two surplices, but very old and shabby' but he was hopeful of a 'speedy reform'. The above quotations are taken from a manuscript volume bearing the title 'An Exact and Impartial Account of the State of the Parishes, Churches, and Parsonage Houses in the Deanery of the 3rd Part of Brecon . . . Taken at the Visitation of Henry Thomas Payne, Rural Dean . . . 1785'.

Not many rural deaneries have so detailed an account of the state of the churches, close on two hundred years ago, accompanied also by a pencil sketch of the churches as they then appeared. For more detailed information about the life and the services of Henry Thomas Payne to the church, the Eisteddfod and his county generally, see my bicentenary article in *Brycheiniog,* the Journal of the Brecknock Society, Vol.V, 1959.

Though separated by close on two hundred years his duties and mine, as rural deans, were in general identical, but I had not to enquire into the due and proper performance of the services. This I would scorn to do for to my personal knowledge the services were most regularly and reverently rendered. Clergy and churchwardens were most careful in noting defects in the roofs of the churches, or any deterioration in the fabric. The linen, including the surplices, the altar, the frontals and the flowers are now generally left to the ladies of the parish, and it would be an occurrence of surprise and comment today if one came across linen 'much stained' or surplices 'very old and shabby'.

Today all the church services in Llanelly parish are in English; in 1785 Payne says they were held in Welsh and English alternately, and as there were two services on a Sunday, the morning and the afternoon congregations were evenly treated. Why so much English at this early date, I cannot understand, for the parish remained virtually Welsh-speaking until the middle of the last century, unless the English was a concession to the gentry families in the bottom part of the parish, along the Usk, who were now being rapidly anglicised, and possibly also to newcomers at the Clydach ironworks — a works established in 1616. In this respect it is worthy of note that the church was extended by the building of the North aisle ten years later, a fact which seems to indicate the arrival of an influx of newcomers.

In winter, the services from Michaelmas to Easter were held only once a Sunday — most certainly in the morning — and again very probably alternately so as to hold the scales even between the two languages. Holy Communion was celebrated three times a year: at Easter, Whitsunday and the first Sunday in November, nor does Payne suggest that it is too infrequent.

Readers may be surprised to learn that an evening service was an innovation that did not establish itself in some districts until comparatively recent times. It was not before 1816, and during the curacy of the Rev. David Rowland that an evening service, 'with the permission of the Bishop' was introduced to St Peter's Church, Carmarthen. In the parish of Bangor Teify until the early years of this century the morning service was the only service of the day — and what a service it was! Men who had attended it told me that if you were not in church half an hour before time you would not get a seat. The principal reason why evening services were not adopted in the country was of course the fact that travelling through dark lanes and over uneven paths was a difficult task if not at times a risky matter. Then again if and when folks got there it would be to a badly-lit church, cold and damp. Nonconformists were, I believe, the first to introduce them generally, and as a result gained an advantage over the church in many places. Morning services, and especially morning funerals, which is still the practice out in Welsh Wales, point to a long tradition going back to medieval times.

What clearly horrified the eighteenth-century Rural Dean was the prevalence of the practice of burying the dead inside the church, an honour which so many Welshmen claimed. He writes: 'I am sorry to observe . . . a custom adopted by the pride of the country in burying their dead within the churches . . . The graves are . . . so often overfilled, that there is scarcely earth sufficient to cover the dead. The Rev. Howell Jones, curate of Llanfeigan . . . declared that he had often times been obliged to quit the church in the midst of divine service, being quite overcome with the stench from the putrid carcasses'.

Another thing that was equally abhorrent to his nature was the existence of 'common charnels where the bones of the deceased have been for years past, piled up in a corner of the churchyard, from whence they are too often idly removed and left scattered, to be bandied by boys, or to the disgrace of humanity, to be gnawed by dogs'. Clearly a great improvement has taken place in the general refinement and in the moral conscience of the countryman since Henry Thomas Payne wrote those words. He has so many interesting things to say that I make no apology at all for quoting at length his description of customs, clothes and cooking as he noticed them amongst his people. These have never before seen the light of day except in that article, already referred to, which I contributed to *Brycheiniog*.

Why he never tried to have any of his manuscripts published is a mystery, unless the secret is given by Theophilus Jones, the historian of Breconshire, who in his preface to that work pays tribute to him 'as one whose talents were much better calculated to ... record the events here treated of ... (but for) a determination on the part of that friend not to appear before the public'. In fact, he was a very shy man.

In one of the manuscripts, I came across this description of the parish wakes, the *gwyl mabsant* which was going strong at this time: 'I had the satisfaction of being present at this grand gala at Llanbedr. The wake is on a Sunday when the church is absolutely thronged with visitors from all the surrounding parishes, dressed out in their best attire, and looking forward with pleasure to the ensuing day, which according to ancient custom is devoted to festivity. The morning is usually spent in rural and athletic sports, and the night in dancing. Long tables are set out in the churchyard for their entertainment, which commences about six o'clock in the evening. From thence they retire to the ball-room at the public house. Then the mantling bliss of *cwrw* is cheerily pledged, and every happy soul is exhilarated by the music of the viol and the harp'. Old Wales enjoying itself! Scenes such as this must have also been enacted every year at Llanelly church for which the ball-room of the Five Bells would come in very handy. What the Llanelly of my day with its eleven chapels would think of it, I don't know. Very significantly, Payne never mentions any chapel or any of the denominations. Methodism must not have taken root in the parish, though we know that there were here many of the schools of Griffith Jones. There were no Romanists in the parish according to his testimony, but there were some Anabaptists and Dissenters 'who frequented their conventicles in parishes adjoining'.

To help us to visualize the better this gay scene, here is his description of the clothes they wore. 'Blue, brown, or striped cloth, home-spun, and woven in the neighbourhood, made into a jacket, waistcoat and lower garments open at the knees, with hose of coarse yarn, forms the common dress . . . And I understand that within these twenty years, red flannel shirts, neatly stitched about the neck and the wrist-bands with white thread, were in universal use among them. Even now they are sometimes seen . . . The women, particularly the elder, wear loose gowns of cloth, with striped or plaided flannel petticoats and checked aprons — coloured handkerchiefs over their necks and shoulders. Broad felt hats with shallow crowns and blue and black yarn stockings — and to this . . . add red flannel shifts . . . The younger females . . . cut a smart appearance with their white kerchiefs and aprons, scarlet cloth cloaks edged with fur, neat mob caps plaited and fastened under the chin with coloured ribbons — and men's round beaver hats . . . They have generally good healthy complexions and small white teeth which they are very careful of'. Such would be the dress also in Llanelly parish at this time.

As these two parishes, Llanbedr and Llanelly, face each other across the Usk and partake — especially at that time — of the same character, his description of the houses would apply equally to both: 'The farm buildings . . . are generally arranged in a line — and the habitations of men and cattle under one common roof. A wide passage commonly separates the cow-house from the kitchen . . . with a porch at the principal entrance . . . The dwelling . . . consists of a spacious kitchen — out of which are two small rooms — one of which is a bed-chamber, and the other a pantry. The room above is frequently used as a common bed-chamber for the whole family — the Master and Mistress sleeping on a raised bed-stead — and the servants on flock mattresses on the floor round the room . . . The farm boys often sleep over the cow-house . . . The windows (of the cottages) are furnished with lattices made of split willow instead of glass, which is seldom seen in such dwellings'.

Having seen how our people enjoyed themselves at the end of the eighteenth century, especially on the occasion of the wakes, and seen how they dressed, and in what sort of houses they lived, I will round off these quotations with his description of their food: 'they keep a pig and the farmers give them (i.e, the cottagers) a little patch of ground . . . to clear for potatoes . . . The farmers salt their own beef and bacon and have their small ale or cyder provided for their harvest; but fleshmeat from the market is a luxury which they seldom indulge in, excepting perhaps at the christening of their children. Bread and cheese with milk flummery and potatoes constituting the common food of this laborious class of people . . . Their bread is commonly made into thin, broad cakes which they term Bara-Llechwen, from its being baked on stones placed over the fire — Llechwen signifies a white flat stone, but iron plates have now . . . superseded the ancient baking-stones', a mode which he condemns as it occasions much waste of flour.

As I said, I make no apology for quoting my predecessor on these matters, for it is not often — I cannot think of any at the moment — that we get so clear a description of the homes, houses, clothes and food of country people at the end of the eighteenth century. It is somewhat of a disappointment to find no mention of the tall hat which we had all along been made to understand was the traditional head-gear of the women of Wales.

In 1959 I was made an Honorary Canon of the Cathedral, an honour which brought me great pleasure, as it was bestowed upon me by a church that knew well my life and work. It brought some confusion to my mind when I retired, for I was not quite sure whether I was entitled to it after that, though when it was bestowed upon me there was no hint that it was a temporary honour. So I wrote to the bishop — bishops are accustomed to have to solve tricky problems, though I am sure he had not met with this one before. He would have no precedents he could fall back on, nor guide-lines he could consult, so he, wisely, passed the problem back to me, informing me, very kindly, that I could do as I liked. If we Honorary Canons present our bishops with difficult problems of this kind, I shall not be surprised if more of them will decide — as I have heard one bishop has already determined — not to make any more of us. The Bishop would be as horrified to suggest as I would be to receive it, that I call myself *Emeritus:* The Reverend, Canon D. Parry-Jones, late Rector of Llanelly, Honorary Canon Emeritus! It looks horrible in print, and it sounds as bad on the lips. It would, of course, be one way of solving it, and one that would be in keeping with a practice that has snowballed into gigantic proportions in the Anglican church of late. At one time, it was moderately used and was confined to the Law, the Church and the Universities, and the recipients were expected by way of justification to offer in return a course of lectures or occupy themselves in some special study. Its random conferment must confuse the ordinary man who may well conclude, that, coming last, on the analogy of academic degrees, it is a higher honour, even dwarfing a doctorate!

Where is it all going to stop, and what's to prevent its being adopted by other bodies, institutions and authorities! We have seen instances of this before, for example, the title of 'professor' has been adopted by propagators or teachers of obscure sciences and cults. Yes, what is to prevent a farmer who wishes to honour a faithful farm servant on his retirement from declaring John Jones, late cowman of the Havod Farm to be henceforth 'John Jones, Cowman Emeritus'! Or who can deny to a local authority the right of dubbing one of its faithful employees: 'David Davies, late of the Tredwr Council, Pest-Officer Emeritus'. And what, again, is to prevent women from claiming the honour — we may yet see some such announcement as this: 'Betty Lewis, late of the *Fun and Feathers,* Bar-tender Emerita'.

I have said a lot about visiting, the primary purpose of which should be — and I tried to keep that always in mind — to keep in touch with our people, to talk about the church and its services, to enquire about attendance at Sunday school, to take a real interest in the careers of our young people, some of whom would be found to be called up to the army, others leaving for college, or, tragically, as during the greater part of my ministry, young people going across the border to look for work and to be lost forever to their families, their country and their church — to try in such cases to advise and cheer. In all ways to share in the joys and griefs of our people.

Not all visits fell into this category, beyond the common purpose of keeping touch. For example, when visiting older members, something in the course of the conversation may have been said to arouse the curiosity of the visitor, or he may have seen something that attracted his attention: One day I was visiting in one of the top hamlets of the parish when I happened to look more closely at a framed, printed document, hanging up above the fireplace. I was immediately intrigued for it was an extraordinary document, indeed a *letter,* purported to have been written by our Lord Jesus Christ and found under a huge stone on Calvary. I was tremendously excited for I had never heard of such a thing in my life. I knew our Lord never wrote anything except a word or two which he wrote in the sand. Later on, in the afternoon, I called at another house in the same hamlet and naturally mentioned this letter, only to be told 'Rector, I've got one of those'. And indeed she had, not framed as with Mrs V. but folded up and put away in a drawer. Mrs Ll. W. told me that hers had been given her by her grandmother (who lived in Ledbury, Gloucestershire) when she came to Wales, and charged to read it often, and especially when she was tempted to do something which she knew was wrong. There is no doubt that this letter was held by Mrs Ll. W. with much the same regard and reverence as she held the New Testament, and she referred to it as *The First Lords Prayer.* I mentioned this letter to a large number of Welsh people but nobody seemed to have heard of it, and I doubt very much whether at any time it had any considerable circulation out in West and Welsh Wales. English copies had apparently been readily available in the valleys of Monmouthshire — printing offices keeping copies in stock.

Mrs V. referred to it as *Our Saviour's Letter* and said that to obtain the maximum benefit from it, it had to be carried on the person, preferably folded up and placed on or near the heart. Hung up, as here, in the home, it gave protection to it and to all who lived in it.

There is nothing in the letter that one can seriously object to, except that it is not what it professes to be, a letter written by Our Lord Jesus Christ. Here is a copy of the letter, including the preamble which explains how it was discovered and how it was preserved.

'Copy of a Letter written by our Blessed Lord and Saviour, Jesus Christ.

'Found 18 miles from Iconium, 63 years after our Blessed Saviour's Crucifixion, transmitted from the Holy City by a converted Jew. Faithfully translated from the original Hebrew Copy, now in the possession of Lady Cuba's family in Mesopotamia. This Letter was written by Jesus Christ, and found under a great stone, round and large, at the foot of the Cross. Upon the stone was engraved 'Blessed is he that turneth me over'.

'All people who saw it prayed earnestly to God and entreated that He would be pleased to make known to them the meaning of this writing that they might not attempt in vain to turn it over.

'In the meantime, there came a little child, about six or seven years old, and turned it over without assistance, to the admiration of every person standing by.

'Under the stone was found this letter written by Jesus Christ. It was carried to Iconium, and there was written 'The Commandments of Jesus Christ', signed by the Angel Gabriel, 74 years after our Saviour's birth.

'Whosoever worketh on the Sabbath day shall be cursed. I command you to go to church, and keep the Lord's day holy, without doing any manner of work. You shall not idly spend your time in bedecking yourselves with superfluities of costly apparel and vain dresses; for I have ordained it a day of rest; I will have the day kept holy, that your sins be forgiven you. You shall not break my commandments, but observe and keep them. Write them in your hearts and steadfastly observe that this was written with my own hand and spoken with my own mouth. You shall not only go to church yourself, but also send your menservants and your maidservants; and observe my word and learn my commandments. You shall finish your labour every Saturday in the afternoon by six o'clock, at which time the preparation for the Sabbath begins. I advise you to fast five Fridays in every year, beginning with Good Friday, and continuing the four Fridays immediately following, in remembrance of the five bloody wounds which I received for all mankind.

'You shall diligently and peacefully labour in your respective callings, wherein it has pleased God to call you. You shall love one another with brotherly love; and cause them that are baptised to come to church and receive the sacrament of the Lord's supper and be made members of the church; and in so doing, I will give you long life and many blessings; your land shall flourish, and your cattle bring forth in abundance; and I will give you many blessings and support in the greatest temptations.

'He that doeth the contrary shall be unprofitable, and I will send a hardness of heart upon them till I see them, but especially, upon the impenitent and unbelievers. He that hath given to the poor shall not be unprofitable. Remember to keep holy the Sabbath day; for the seventh day I have taken unto myself. He that hath a copy of this letter, written with my own hand and spoken with my own mouth, and keepeth it without publishing it to others, shall not prosper; but he that publisheth it to others shall be blessed of me; and though his sins in number be as the stars of the sky, if he believes in this, they shall be pardoned; but if he believes not this writing and this commandment, I will send many plagues upon him and consume both him, and his children, and his cattle.

'And whosoever shall have a copy of this letter written

with my own hand, and keep it in their houses, nothing shall hurt them — neither lightning, pestilence, nor thunder. And if a woman be with child, and in labour, she shall be safely delivered of her birth. You shall not have any tidings of me, but by the holy scriptures, until the day of judgements. All goodness, happiness and prosperity shall be in the house where a copy of this letter shall be found'.

The letter was certainly spurious and mischievous, and ought to be preached against and shown up for what it really was, but as I discovered only two in the parish and further discovered from my correspondence that it was extremely rare, I decided not to give it any publicity, but entirely to ignore it.

I got into touch with libraries and individuals whom I knew to be interested in such things, amongst them, Dr Iorwerth C. Peate, the Curator of the Welsh Folk Museum at St Fagans who informed me that it was known in Wales as the *Llythyr dan Garreg* (the letter under the stone) and that Welsh translations of it were extant. He and I — taking the two letters with me — appeared in a brief programme on B.B.C. television, and discussed the possible extent to which it was known to the Welsh peasantry.

When I retired, one of the first things I did was to write out and put in some kind of order the thousands of notes of all kinds I had made in the course of my twenty-six years as Rector of Llanelly. When writing up the story of this letter, it occurred to me that it would be interesting to find out if there were any more of them about, so I put a letter in the local paper, and very interesting replies were received. One copy came from Mrs North, in Newport; this had a great deal more in it than the one I had discovered in my own parish. It contained a letter which King Agbarus is supposed to have written to our Saviour, and our Saviour's reply. It contained also a physical description of our Redeemer, which, I must say I liked very much and could wish it was true. Indeed, I wondered whether it was not possible for a picture, or a description of his face and person to have been handed down in tradition and folk memory, especially in such a close-knit community as that of his followers, committed as they were to keep alive all that was known of him and all that he said. Such a face — such a personality — that had captivated and enthralled so many that had gazed upon it, could surely have lived on in folk memory for many generations, as the relationship was so uniquely personal, where in work and suffering and prayer that face was ever before them as their strength and inspiration. I tried by all means to convince myself that it could be true. Tradition is a very real and persistent thing, and can live on in folk memory for generations. But was there any basis in tradition for it? The person, or persons, who had invented the letter were capable of inventing anything! Of course one had to abandon every possibility of its having any credibility whatsoever — hard as it was, for he was made out to have auburn hair, and I belong to a pocket, or tribe, of people who have red or auburn hair!

I had two or three more copies from the valleys of Monmouthshire, one of which was published by Samuel and John Keys, Devonport, sold also at Stone's Stationery Establishment, 10 Fore Street, Exeter, and by W. Burridge, Truro. In no case did any of my informants say or hint that it was ever used as a charm. Well, here is that part which gives a description of the person of our Saviour.

'There appeared in these our days a man of great virtue, called Jesus Christ, who, by the people, is called a prophet; but his disciples call him the Son of God. He raiseth the dead; and cures all manner of diseases, a man of stature, somewhat tall and comely, with a reverend countenance, such as the beholders both fear and love. His hair is of the colour of a chestnut all ripe, and is plain almost down to his ears, but from thence downward, is somewhat curled, but more of the oriental colour, waving about his shoulders; in the middle of his head is a seam or parting, like the Nazarites. His forehead very plain and smooth. His face without either wrinkle or spot, beautiful with a comely red, his nose and mouth so formed that nothing can be reprehended; his beard thick, the colour of his hair on his head; his eyes grey, clear, and quick. In reproving he is severe; in counselling he is courteous; he is of a fair-spoken, pleasant and grave speech; never seen by anyone to laugh, but often seen by many to weep; in proportion to his body, he is well-shaped and straight; and both hands and arms are very delectable. In speaking, he is very temperate, modest and wise. A man for his singular beauty, far exceeding all the sons of men'.

Later on I sought more evidence about it and about its origin.

In the *Encyclopaedia of Religion and Ethics* it states that 'within Christianity, one of the earliest mentions of a celestial "letter" occurs in the . . . second half of the second century'. To this category 'belongs the very interesting "letter" for the hallowing of Sunday (our Saviour's letter), whose history may be traced back at least to the sixth century, and which has spread, despite many efforts to check it, throughout both Western and Eastern Christendom.

'Although much study has been devoted to this letter, its history is by no means clear. The earliest known mention of the "Sunday letter" is its condemnation as a diabolical forgery, by Lucinianus, bishop of Carthage, towards the end of the sixth century . . .'

Originally, the 'letter' emphasises the keeping of Sunday, but later it came to insist on other duties as well. It often concluded with maledictions on the disobedient and unbelieving, but some specimens also contain a benediction on those who do its bidding.

'With the addition of a blessing for obeying the commands of the heavenly "letter", the way was open for what is today the most important function of the epistle — its use as an amulet to ward off all harm'.

Its origin 'is West, not East, and, in all probability, Africa or Spain'.

Still, I am of the opinion that to most of the pious people of Wales of the last century it was valued for what it made out it was — and there lay its danger.

I found the parish full of memories of the appearances and workings of the supernatural, full of the tales of magic and witchcraft, full of folk tales about pools and wells and standing stones, full, too, of the wonderful cures effected by charmers in the human as well as in the animal field. Of the dozen or so of charmers that seem to have existed at the beginning of the century, the most famous seems to have been Solomon Chilton. There were others who coveted the honour and the power, men who believed they had been endowed with the necessary gift and who had tried out their hand at it, but had never made the grade. Chilton's way of dealing with a lame beast was to watch where he put his foot down, cut the mark of the hoof out, put in in a thorn bush, and as the wind and the rain worked on it, until it disintegrated, so, by means of sympathetic magic, would the animal improve; cure being achieved when the clod finally crumbled away. This cure has been applied to lame cattle since the last World War!

We must disabuse our minds of certain ideas that we may have formed in these more enlightened years that these men were at bottom rogues, exploiting the credulity and ignorance of an earlier age. Nothing of the kind! They were men who genuinely believed they had been endowed with this gift and that it was their duty and privilege therefore to put it at the disposal of the community. Though they received small rewards, they never made a charge. Allied with them were the men who had the gift to set bones — often believed to be hereditary, as indeed were the gifts of the charmer, and cases are known where those who had specialised in stopping bleeding had begged of one of the sons to submit himself to the art or discipline. But in almost all cases the young men would have nothing to do with it, much to the sorrow of their parents.

It must be remembered that these men flourished in an age when there was no doctor or veterinary surgeon nearer than the county town and whereas it might take an hour to get there and another to come back, the charmer was at the next farm and could be reached in ten minutes. In that interval the life of an animal or a man could be in danger unless attended to immediately. I am thinking now more especially of those who possessed the power to stop bleeding and many wonderful instances were related to me by reliable and responsible men.

I heard tales of men and animals bewitched, and how

farmers put branches of the elder tree over the stable door, especially on the first of May, to prevent the witches entering and taking out the horses to ride them; of how the elder was almost regarded as a sacred tree, and how young men were taught never to cut down an elder tree without first taking their cap off to it. Bits of the elder and the wittan tree were carried in their pockets by men to protect them from the wiles of wicked fairies and witches. Housewives chalked their doorsteps after a certain pattern that allowed no nick or gap, however small, or otherwise a witch would find her way in.

One day, sick-visiting in the top end of the parish, I found in one house the old lady moaning in pity for her poor husband who wanted to die, but couldn't. I asked her why, 'Because' she said, 'he's lying on a feather bed'. I tried to reason with her and console her, that when his time came, the good Lord would take him out of his misery, but she would have none of it. In the end, with elderly people, I never tried to argue against, or demolish, a belief, a conviction, long held, which, however mistaken, had given their life some sort of stability and, possibly, at times, solace and comfort. I talked to many women who as young girls, for a bit of fun, had tried to find out who loved them by means of the key and the Bible.

A man in Crickhowell told me that a few years before he had bought some cattle from an old lady on the Black Mountains, and while there fancied a flowering plant, which she said he could have, but he refused to accept it for nothing, saying that he would give her half-a-crown for it, but that he hadn't it on him that moment. He planted it at the bottom of the garden and it throve well — and he forgot the half-a-crown. When he went to that part of the garden next the plant was drying up and obviously dying. Soon he met the old lady and gave her the half-a-crown, but did not like to tell her that the plant was withering and dying. However, in late Spring the following year he and his wife went down to that part of the garden and lo and behold! the plant was putting forth new buds and showing vigorous signs of new life and growth. 'I am sure' he said 'that old Magw put a spell on that plant until she got her money!'

There were tales of standing stones: one which had been a

farmer, but who, owing to his cruelty to his wife, had been turned into a stone and was destined ever after to go down each mid-summer night to the pool in the Usk, where she had drowned herself, to beg of her to come back. The 'Lonely shepherd' was a well-known and much-loved tall pillar of lime rock, standing guard over the parish, from its pitch high on the escarpment overlooking the vale below. Every mid-summer night he went through the vale counting his sheep. He was much visited and was known to be whitewashed so that he could the more easily be seen.

I was shown a fairy ring in a delightful spot above the valley mists, ideal for dancing on moonlit nights. Above it was the 'long man's grave' *(bedd y gwr hir)* a giant of ten foot, but whose body was found to have grown two feet since he was buried.

There were men hardly past the middle age who as children, for the cure of hernia, had been passed through a split ash, even younger men who had been cured of pneumonia by following the old treatment of having sheep's lungs put to their feet — a case of this was discovered in Gwent as late as 1960! More had gone through one of the many bizarre treatments for whooping cough, including that of being swung round by the heel in the famous Llangattock caves.

Many people are as interested in how legends start as in the legends themselves. Well, I can say how one started, for it had its origin in one of our churchyards, and was rapidly spreading during the quarter of a century I was Rector of the parish. In this particular yard (the Gilwern yard) there lies on the tomb of the late Colonel Sandeman the carved figure of a big white dog which attracts much attention, for visitors to church-yards are familiar with figures of angels and doves in such places, but not dogs. And as the human mind, like nature, abhors a vacuum, that is, unanswered questions and unresolved mysteries, it begins to work on the few facts it can discover (the fewer the better, as too many can only encumber the imagination). This is how the legend stood when I left the parish in 1961:

On the day Colonel Sandeman was buried, his faithful dog

followed his coffin all the way to the grave, and when friends and mourners turned away the dog remained! Every day the dog went to the grave, many a time had it been seen lying there, many a time late at night, and again at early dawn as workers passed on their way to their early shift. However, one morning after a cold, wintry night of frost and snow, he was found where he now lies in effigy, cold and stiff, and dead! He was buried by the side of his master.

The man who told me this story was a native of Abertillery, where he had heard it thirty years before.

Many visitors come today to visit this grave and to stare in admiration and affection at the marble figure of this faithful and devoted dog. Such a story was bound to arise — for such a story must be true, else what is a dog doing on his master's tombstone?

Not only dog-lovers, but men in general were ready for a new dog story. They had been served with the story of Gelert, Llywellyn's dog, for over seven hundred years and it was getting a little bit stale by now, but here, at last, in this carved figure, with its few moving and pathetic facts, they found it.

I found some corroboration for the story of the nightly visits of this dog from a Clydach man who, during the depression, used to do a little poaching. In order to avoid the road on the way home he used to go over the stile below the churchyard and through the fields. However, every time he passed this way his dog became nervous and alert, and many a time he saw the shadow of a dog moving away towards the graves. He was convinced it was the colonel's dog.

I long hesitated to set the story down in writing, in case it was accepted as the legend in its final form, for it is capable of very considerable amplification and embellishment yet, which I hope it will have, and, left to the curious and inventive minds of the ordinary people, I am sure it will.

These tales were just behind us — at our heels, and I thought I ought to preserve as many of them as I could, for they witness to what at different times occupied, and indeed influenced the minds of country people. They show too, how tenacious folk memory is.

This is pre-eminently the age of the collector, and varied indeed are the objects collected — I loved to collect old lore. In some instances it took some patience and not a little ingenuity to get information out of people, especially out of those who mistakenly believed that, as religious people, they should regard them as beneath their interest and only with shame to admit they ever listened to them. One way was to show one's own interest in them, then refer to Sir John Rhys's immense work in this field — his example carried great weight — and above all to try to show them — and it never failed to work — that in this particular field they had the knowledge, they were the teachers, we were the seekers, the learners, making it quite clear at the same time that we never for one moment thought they believed in any of them.

All this shows how conservative the human mind is, how retentive folk memory, and how hard old attitudes of mind, old beliefs and customs die, and as an illustration of this, in an earlier age, I will quote what my predecessor Henry Thomas Payne, says of a woman whose conduct he watched as she came down to bathe in one of the healing wells of the parish. He might be describing something that must have happened in the middle ages and not something that was seen well over three hundred years after the Reformation.

'The following instance of superstitious faith upon this head actually occurred within my own observation about three years ago (that would be between 1785 and 1793), when, as I was riding with a friend up the railroad, on the opposite side of the Clydach from the well, I observed an old woman descending by a dangerously steep path from the summit of the mountain to the dingle. Where it was possible for her to do it with safety, she stopped, and spent a few minutes upon her knees with her hands clasped together, seemingly in fervent prayer. This was repeated several times in the course of the descent.

'At length, having reached the bottom, she devoutly crossed herself, knelt down, and seemed to pray with great agitation for about a quarter of an hour. She then took off her shoes and stockings, neckerchief and cap, walked into the water of the well, and stooping down, threw it backwards over her head. Afterwards she washed her face, neck and head, as well as her feet, and concluded the ceremony by a long prayer upon her knees before she dressed herself. Having accomplished the object of her pilgrimage, she returned by the same way that she came, kneeling at certain distances as before.

'The ceremony of crossing and throwing water backward over her head, as I have since learned, was intended to counteract the malicious power of certain evil spirits who are supposed to inhabit the recesses of a neighbouring dingle, which mixes its waters with the Clydach, called Cwm-Pwca, or the Hobgoblins Dingle, of whom the neighbouring peasants, even to the present day, entertain a considerable dread. Shakespeare's Puck is evidently grounded upon the Welsh name — he is, in fact the same'.

Over two hundred years later a young girl told me that her grandmother taught them whenever they entered church to bow to the altar and bend the knee. In the secluded valleys and odd corners of Wales, very old beliefs and old practices have survived.

TWELVE

Retirement

———◦———

I WAS NOW NEARING my seventieth birthday and as I was still healthy and strong, I had not given much thought to retiring at all, but my wife reminded me of my age and said that I ought to retire; that with our state and church pension we could manage very well, so I had to think very seriously about it. Things would not get easier for me; for the last ten years I had worked alone, my three old faithful lay-readers had gone, but I had had a car for many years, a boon which, in a parish such as Llanelly where long distances ate up time and sapped energy, enabled me to do the work of a curate as well. For many years too I had introduced a Sunday bus to gather the people from the top end of the parish right down to Gilwern for the evening service at the parish church. It could well be one of the first experiments of this kind in the British Isles, certainly in Wales, for I had not heard of another at that time.

What decided me finally to call it a day was the thought that my wife had, for nearly the whole of our married life, had to run very big houses, and since the war, without the help of a maid. She, too, had to be considered. The first thing we did was to go and see some clergy flats down at Llandaff. In this matter I relied entirely upon the advice and decision of my wife. But we did not like any of them: they seemed something quickly thrown up, without much imagination and indeed with very little consideration, for many of them had flights of stairs to them — one with three long flights of steps, up to the very attic, and that for elderly clergy!

Neither I nor my wife had been accustomed to look far

into the future but we had to do so now. That's why we had
been frightened by the long flights of steps at Llandaff, and
that is one reason why we tried to look for a flat at Newport
— we had a daughter living there. The other reason was that I
felt I could offer a good many years' service to the church
yet, and wished therefore to stay within the Province. This
second, voluntary stretch of service lasted for exactly ten
years and a very happy term of service it was, for one was
made so welcome in all the churches. I could not help
contrasting it with what could happen half a century earlier,
especially in the case of curates, when they were much more
numerous — and much cheaper. Verily, scarcity had worked
wonders! For a once fully-staffed parish, now sadly depleted
in man-power, to see an ordained priest coming along to take
the service was an occasion for congratulation and welcome.

In those ten years one had one or two curious experiences:
In one church on Easter Day, I found a large and beautiful
Prayer Book on the Altar and I just glanced to see if it was
opened at the right day — and it was. As we were getting to
the end of the first hymn, I began to turn the leaves to get
ready to begin the service, and just to make sure took
another casual look at the collect, and to my astonishment it
was not the collect for Easter Day at all, nor upon
examination, were the epistle and gospel those for the day. I
began to turn leaves, but to no purpose and I became quite
flustered. The hymn was now finished and yet I was turning
leaves and trying to find my way about. Anyhow, I could
wait no longer, so I turned to the congregation and asked if
someone would kindly supply me with an ordinary Prayer
Book, and a man held up his hand. As he handed me the
book he whispered 'It is the wife's Prayer Book'. When he
said that I wondered whether I had fallen from the frying-pan
into the fire, for I had never heard of a Prayer Book for
wives, but when he added, again in a whisper, that it was a
Girl Guide Prayer Book, I knew I had, for I had never heard
of that either. However, I had a quick look at it and found
that it had at any rate the proper collect, epistle and gospel,
and that it began in the ordinary way, so I gradually calmed
down and the service went from there on without a hitch.
After the service was over I took the book from the altar and

had a good look at it — it was an English version of the *Use of Sarum*.

The other experience was in a church, again outside Newport. On entering the pulpit here, I had a bit of a shock — a mild shock — which in retrospect provided me with much food for thought, culminating in a resolution to pass on this experience, or shock, for the benefit of others, for I believe that, though it was only a symbol, it spoke volumes to those, who, like me, make use of the pulpit. As I ascended the steps into this particular pulpit, I noticed it had been boarded with asbestos sheets. 'My word' I said to myself 'they expect fire in this pulpit, and have made every preparation for it.'

As I thought of it afterwards if occurred to me what a good thing it would be if every pulpit was lined with asbestos if only to remind the preacher that the church expected the gospel to be preached with Pentecostal fire, as on that famous day in Jerusalem, and by one burning with conviction and on fire with the urgency of his message. Some years later, I read in the *Church Times* of a vicar's instruction to his *locum* that if he needed the hose, he would find it in the pulpit, meaning of course that if he wished to water the garden he would know where to find it. I think that all pulpits should be lined with asbestos or, failing that, have a length of hose coiled up in them as a perpetual challenge, and a constant reminder of the Day of Pentecost, for there is nothing calculated to push us down into the slough of boredom and misery more than to sit under a preacher who gives us the impression that he couldn't care less whether he is heard or not, whether he is understood, or whether he goes on with his sermon or not.

One of the tasks that comes the way of all clergy is that of burning old sermons. It is not an easy task, and is one that is put off till the very last moment. It is hard to throw on the burning heap sermons that one thought a lot of, whose message had gone forth more than once and from more than one pulpit. The occasion of its writing may come back and a fleeting memory of the enthusiasm under which it was composed may return to make one wish he could hold his hand, but the job has to be done and one cannot give in to sentiment or any other feeling. It is true they contain golden thoughts and inspired words and visions, or so one thought, but these visions and inspired words were not wasted, they were supplied for immediate use, while they were fresh and oven-hot. As I intended to offer my services on Sundays to the diocese of Monmouth, I kept a few of those which I thought would be most useful, not necessarily those that contained the nuggets, but I might as well have destroyed these too, for I made hardly any use of them as the fashion in preaching was changing so very rapidly — one just fixed on a thought in the collect, epistle or gospel and expanded on that for a quarter of an hour or so.

After ten years of Sunday help in a dozen churches and more in the diocese of Monmouth, I had to call it a day, not that I wasn't physically equal to the task, but because of the return of an old trouble that hit me twenty-five years previously — miniere's disease, a malady that affects the middle ear, causing loss of balance and making everything in front of one rise and fall like the swelling of the sea. It is a frightening experience and I became afraid it might take me in the pulpit or worse still, at the altar, and I had prided myself that in over half a century I had never had an accident with the cup, a thing that could easily happen, as with unaccustomed sleeves such as those of the surplice, one false move would be quite sufficient. I suppose every priest has lived with that horror somewhere in the wide margin of his conscious thinking all his life. I wanted to keep my record.

To return to my departure from Llanelly parish, a presentation was made to me and my wife and very nice things were said. It all made it easier to part with people whom I had known and with whom I had identified myself for a quarter of a century. It was obvious at last that those who were nearest to me in my work believed — a most difficult thing to convince anybody of in Wales — that I had been a busy man.

As we were going into a flat, a large portion of the furniture had to be sold. To part with sticks that had been with us since we started our life together and which were the constant reminders of the thrill which marked their arrival — after much hard saving — was not easy.

For me, it was as hard to part with my books as with my sermons, but they had to go, and tied up in bundles of twelve, they were sold off for two shillings — just twopence per volume! Neither of us went to the sale.

We were both young enough to feel once again the thrill of going into a new home and to start quite a new life — at last, one without any responsibility to anybody for anything except ourselves. We have both of us been very happy in retirement, I in that I have at last all the time in the world to read and to write, and my wife in that she has a modern kitchen where everything is within reach, electricity for cooking and gas to provide the central heating.

After eight years of real happiness, much of which came to us with watching our grandchildren growing up and developing, for my wife was a great family person — the blow fell. She had been up in her beloved Cheshire spending a holiday with her sister and I was meeting her at the station on her return. We caught the bus for home and were sitting side by side talking away gaily — she saying what a nice time she had had and I answering questions as to how I had fared while she was away. Then out of the corner of my eye I could see that her eyes were closed, and upon turning fully round I was in time to catch her limp head coming to rest on my shoulder — and she was dead.

Of the changes that I have seen in the church since I was ordained, one is the comparatively recent discovery of the layman. He does not seem to have counted for much in the past, not much even at the commencement of this century, and as far as he himself was concerned he was quite happy to let it remain so. The church had never been able to do without him quite — he was necessary to make a congregation — so that the priest might have somebody to preach to; at one time, in the earlier days of Methodism, if the preacher was in the mood, someone to harangue and confine to the fires of hell. Apart from that, the church does not seem to have had any particular use for him. But in the increasingly complex nature of modern society, and the resulting problems and tensions, the church — using the term in its then accepted meaning as consisting only of the ordained priesthood in its various orders — found that by its peculiar academic training, consisting mostly of the classics and theology, it was not particularly equipped to deal with these pressing problems. They were the problems of the secular world, the layman's world, problems that he himself was part of and often suffering from. So, tardily, his value was recognised and he was taken into full partnership. The tendency of modern society towards greater secularization has meant that the voice of the pulpit has not been able to reach the masses over the ever-increasing distance that separates them, and here again the church had to call in the layman to help it even in its primary work of evangelization. In the past he had been allowed to hold such posts as that of church-warden. He was handy to organize sales of work, whist drives, concerts and all efforts that might bring in money. But today so important is he in every aspect of church life and activity, especially in its witness to the world, that we may be in danger of going to the other extreme — especially as the emphasis at the moment is on the priesthood of the laity — of looking upon the historic priesthood as merely a necessary adjunct to perform those hereditary functions always associated with it and restricted to it.

The church might well think of establishing an order, such as the Order of Merit, whereby it can suitably honour men who have rendered great service to it. Some way, too, ought to be found to honour women who for many years now have rendered heroic service, especially in the mission field, where they have endured hardships and physical strain we never knew the female frame could stand. In the case of those women who happen to be wives of clergy, the only way of honouring them found so far is to honour the husband, and canons have been made that have caused a whole diocese to raise its eyebrows. Some better way must be found. An order such as that of St Non (mother of Saint David) could be established, and we may yet read of such an appointment as this: Margaret, Dame of the Order of St Non.

One has seen other changes, some of which cannot help causing anxiety as one contemplates the future of the Anglican Communion:- one of them is the virtual eclipse of the sermon as we knew it in the first half of my ministry. A sermon drew hundreds of thousands to our churches on

Sunday to hear the men who had been preparing for them the previous week. What we have today are *chats, talks,* and as is often admitted in prefatory remarks: 'Just a few words', and that is what they are, so simplified and elementary, that they would be scorned in a discussion in an old Welsh Sunday school class. No great theme in Christian belief or conduct is taken. The Anglican church must surely suffer for this one day.

Another change has been the abandonment of pastoral visiting. This must cause grief to those who in a long ministry have seen its value and reaped its benefits. Not so long ago I had a letter from an old priest, well in his eighties, complaining that he never saw any of the clergy: 'they all seem to be too busy' and he must have wondered what with, for like me, he had for the greater part of his life to do his work on foot or on his bicycle. Of course old priests often bore us with telling the same story over and over again, and repeat bits of sermons in which they had been inspired and in which they felt doors had been opened to them to see what no other eye had seen before and no eye will ever see again, but if you tell us: 'Look here now, Dai, I've heard that one before', we shan't mind, for we can fall back on dozens of others that you've heard before!

As the Anglican sermon was so intimately connected with Mattins, it is no wonder that the latter should share its fate and be relegated, where it is retained at all, to a said service and be satisfied with the status and importance of a week-night evensong. Must the worship of Christian people when they gather together to honour their creator take one form only? What is wrong with a service in which a considerable portion of holy scripture is read, apart from psalms and the ancient canticles, and where many causes are prayed for — a service in which the congregation take a greater part than in any other in our Prayer Book? It still holds its own out in Welsh-speaking Wales, but even there, and especially where two or three parishes are amalgamated and where one service only is possible, that tends to be the Holy Communion.

Long used to a Sunday celebration of the Holy Communion, I like it that way, but we should not despise an earlier practice of country churches — shared with all other Christian bodies — of celebrating it only on the first Sunday in the month. Coming only at that interval, it filled a bigger place in the minds of the communicants than it does in the more frequent communions of town churches. It went by its own name of *Cwdd Mawr* — the great service — and it was always preceded in the week before by a preparation service in which the parish priest led us in prayer, and expounded some aspect of its profound meaning and purpose. It was not lightly approached nor lightly received.

I am afraid that another custom of the Welsh churches must disappear with the suppression of the general invitation — 'Ye that do truly' — in the revised Prayer Book, for, here, we all stood up (and in some churches the communicants moved forward to the front of the church, and even to the chancel) while the invitation was being read, meekly kneeling to make our confession. It also made sense, for what was the point in inviting people to kneel who were already on their knees? I was always moved by this symbolic act of rising and moving forward at this juncture and felt that it contributed much to the solemnity of this part of the service where we begin to intensify our preparation for the worthy partaking of the sacrament.

I am in favour of all survivals, especially where, as in the above custom, it can inform the act with deep significance, indeed even in cases where they can have no significance or meaning whatsoever. For example, a custom has survived in the churches of Colva and Bryngwyn, in Breconshire, where the sexes separate themselves at the church door, the women going to sit on the north side and the men on the south; nor do the women move up to take the sacrament until all the men have returned to their places. It was the custom also amongst the Moravians and is not unknown to this day in some Non-conformist churches. I remember one member suggesting, when our own mission church of St James, in the parish of Llangeler, was opened in 1902, that the men and the women should sit on separate sides, but the idea was not taken up.

I do not wish to stray into fields that do not concern me, but there is a trend that I have noticed of recent years, and

that is for some amongst the young to leave the ministry for
secular work, in the social services, in teaching and in
television, a thing unthinkable in my early years. It has not
hit the church quite to the same extent yet. At one time we
all believed — to what ever Christian body we belonged
— that there was no greater honour than to be what we were,
ministers of the gospel. To have turned our backs on the
ministry would then have been regarded as the betrayal of a
sacred vow and profession.

Long ministries in the same parish — even life-long
ministries — are now things of the past though there was a lot
to be said for them. The priest became known and became
accepted as a father amongst his people — and it was
something more than a mere title or form of address. It is an
experience that brings its own reward when a priest marries
those whom he has baptised and starts all over again a new
round of baptisms. It had another advantage in that it would
dishearten the most stubborn member who after a tiff or
misunderstanding with his vicar decided to boycott the
church. The prospect of having to be loyal to his resolution
for forty years — or perhaps even longer — would make the
stoutest heart quail. As one who worked for over a quarter of
a century in one parish, I must say that there are advantages
too in more frequent moves.

When I was young, the generality of church-goers were not
half so well educated as they are today, yet I never heard any
of them complain that they could not understand their New
Testament, or that they could not follow the sermons — and
there was a great deal of profound doctrinal substance in the
old sermons. It is very difficult for me therefore to
understand this modern urge to simplify the language of
scripture and the liturgy and reduce them almost to the level
of colloquial speech. My generation expected the Bible and
the liturgy to have their own vocabulary, their own standards
and their own manner of expression. Unless one draws the
line somewhere, one can render them contemptible. Fortunately for us Welsh-speaking people the common usage of our
language will ever protect us from addressing the Almighty as
'You' — *chwi!*

Another thing that amazes me is the daring of some young

priests in denying vital articles of the Christian faith, such as the virgin birth, the resurrection and even belief in the after-life, and as far as I have been able to find out they have not been disciplined. Are we in for an era of creed-less and god-less religion?

And what is behind the emergence of ancient cults and practices, early discarded by the church, such as speaking with tongues! The considerable patronage the church extends to the presentation of the gospel story in new, dramatic forms presenting sacred scenes with a familiarity and a lack of what we used to know as reverence, puzzles me. There is such a lot that I don't understand — I do not pass judgement, I can only say it was time I retired!

I am glad that while my ministry lasted the Book of Common Prayer remained enthroned as the authoritative voice of the church, revealing its mind and its belief in the manner in which it set out our Sunday services and directed the 'thoughts of our hearts' in our worship of the Almighty. On every page it bore the seal and sanction of its authority. In it we saw the church at the altar, offering; at the font, receiving; at the sick bed, comforting, and at the graveside commending. Through its use our church was seen to be with us at every domestic, social and national occasion.

I don't know that the church, officially, realised how loyally enshrined it was in the hearts of the ordinary church members. Two of my sisters married young men who eventually became — as they were expected to do — deacons in their respective denominations. But as they left home they took their prayer books with them, and one of them, after a membership of over fifty years in her chapel, where she went regularly with her husband and where she took her family, asked me one day if I could get her a large-type prayer book, for the print of the one she treasured all these years was getting too small for her to read with comfort.

In those days, if a man took his prayer book with him he could go into any Anglican church in the empire — or outside the empire — and join in the service whatever the language might be. I remember as a boy, while holidaying with my grandmother, attending evensong at the parish church, Cenarth, and during the confession becoming aware of strange and alien accents in the pew behind me; it kept on right through the recitation of the psalms, the canticles and the versicles. Here was a monoglot lumberman (for there was much tree-felling at that time in the extensive woodlands on the lower reaches of the *Teifi*) joining in the service with us, for though our language differed, he knew that the prayer book carried our thoughts and prayers forward together at every step.

Our prayer book needed modernising, and many of the prayers and services needed shortening. The novelty of new words and expressions will not strike us as forcibly as they will English worshippers, for in our many editions of the Welsh prayer book, archaic words were dropped in favour of newer ones, and outworn expressions modernised — and this we did without reference to Canterbury, Convocation or Parliament. Of course, what we were doing was trying to express more clearly in current Welsh the meaning of the English version, which we took as our standard and authoritative version.

I like the new services, and when they are gathered together in one volume and given the seal of authority by the church, I think the new Book of Common Prayer will take the place of the old in the affections of our people. I trust that the provincial versions will not differ too widely, so that English visitors to our vernacular services may still be able to join in with us in our worship.

I very much like, in our baptismal service, our reference to the child to be baptised as 'this little man', whereas in English he is referred to as 'this infant'. I should not be surprised if I was told that a mother first suggested this as our Welsh equivalent of *infant* — *y dyn bychan yma*, 'this little man'. And the same, *mutatis mutandis,* for the little girl.